Opposing Viewpoints ®

WAR AND HUMAN NATURE

Opposing Viewpoints®

David L. Bender
Bruno Leone

Greenhaven Press

577 Shoreview Park Road
St. Paul, Minnesota 55126

Library of Congress Cataloging-in-Publication Data

Bender, David L. 1936-
    War and human nature.

    (Opposing viewpoints series)
    Includes bibliographies and index.
    1. War—Addresses, essays, lectures. 2. Man—Addresses, essays, lectures. I. Leone, Bruno, 1939-   . II. Title. III. Series.
U21.2.B397 1985   355'.02   85-8008
ISBN 0-89908-341-2 (lib. ed.)
ISBN 0-89908-316-1 (pbk.)

"Congress shall make no law... abridging the freedom of speech, or of the press."

first amendment to the U S Constitution

The basic foundation of our democracy is the first amendment guarantee of freedom of expression. The *Opposing Viewpoints Series* is dedicated to the concept of this basic freedom and the idea that it is more important to practice it than to enshrine it.

Contents

Chapter 4: What Is a War Crime?

Chapter 5: Are Peace Movements Effective?

Why Consider Opposing Viewpoints?

"It is better to debate a question without settling it than to settle a question without debating it."

Joseph Joubert (1754-1824)

The Importance of Examining Opposing Viewpoints

The purpose of this book, and the Opposing Viewpoints Series as a whole, is to confront you with alternative points of view on complex and sensitive issues.

Probably the best way to inform yourself is to analyze the positions of those who are regarded as experts and well studied on the issues. It is important to consider every variety of opinion in an attempt to determine the truth. Opinions from the mainstream of society should be examined. Also important are opinions that are considered radical, reactionary, minority or stigmatized by some other uncomplimentary label. An important lesson of history is the fact that many unpopular and even despised opinions eventually gained widespread acceptance. The opinions of Socrates, Jesus and Galileo are good examples of this.

You will approach this book with opinions of your own on the issues debated within it. To have a good grasp of your own viewpoint you must understand the arguments of those with whom you disagree. It is said that those who do not completely understand their adversary's point of view do not fully understand their own.

Perhaps the most persuasive case for considering opposing viewpoints has been presented by John Stuart Mill in his work *On Liberty*. Consider the following statements of his when studying controversial issues:

> If all mankind minus one were of one opinion, and only one person were of the contrary opinion, mankind would be no

more justified in silencing that one person than he, if he had the power, would be justified in silencing mankind. . . .

We can never be sure that the opinion we are endeavoring to stifle is a false opinion. . . .

All silencing of discussion is an assumption of infallibility. . . .

Ages are no more infallible than individuals; every age having held many opinions which subsequent ages have deemed not only false but absurd; and it is as certain that many opinions now general will be rejected by future ages. . . .

The only way in which a human being can make some approach to knowing the whole of a subject, is by hearing what can be said about it by persons of every variety of opinion, and studying all modes in which it can be looked at by every character of mind. No wise man ever acquired his wisdom in any mode but this.

Pitfalls to Avoid

A pitfall to avoid in considering alternative points of view is that of regarding your own point of view as being merely common sense and the most rational stance, and the point of view of others as being only opinion and naturally wrong. It may be that the opinion of others is correct and that yours is in error.

Another pitfall to avoid is that of closing your mind to the opinions of those whose views differ from yours. The best way to approach a dialogue is to make your primary purpose that of understanding the mind and arguments of the other person and not that of enlightening him or her with your solutions. One learns more by listening than by speaking.

It is my hope that after reading this book you will have a deeper understanding of the issues debated and will appreciate the complexity of even seemingly simple issues when good and honest people disagree. This awareness is particularly important in a democratic society such as ours, where people enter into public debate to determine the common good. People with whom you disagree should not be regarded as enemies, but rather as friends who suggest a different path to a common goal.

Analyzing Sources of Information

The Opposing Viewpoints Series uses diverse sources; magazines, journals, books, newspapers, statements and position papers from a wide range of individuals and organizations. These sources help in the development of a mindset that is open to the consideration of a variety of opinions.

The format of the Opposing Viewpoints Series should help you answer the following questions.

1. Are you aware that three of the most popular weekly news magazines, *Time, Newsweek,* and *U.S. News and World Report,* are not totally objective accounts of the news?
2. Do you know there is no such thing as a completely objective author, book, newspaper or magazine?
3. Do you think that because a magazine or newspaper article is unsigned it is always a statement of facts rather than opinions?
4. How can you determine the point of view of newspapers and magazines?
5. When you read do you question an author's frame of reference (political persuasion, training, and life experience)?

Many people finish their formal education unable to cope with these basic questions. They have little chance to understand the social forces and issues surrounding them. Some fall easy victims to demagogues preaching solutions to problems by scapegoating minorities with conspiratorial and paranoid explanations of complex social issues.

I do not want to imply that anything is wrong with authors and publications that have a political slant or bias. All authors have a frame of reference. Readers should understand this. You should also understand that almost all writers have a point of view. An important skill in reading is to be able to locate and identify a point of view. This series gives you practice in both.

Developing Basic Reading and Thinking Skills

A number of basic skills for critical thinking are practiced in the discussion activities that appear throughout the books in the series. Some of the skills are described below.

Evaluating Sources of Information: The ability to choose from among alternative sources the most reliable and accurate source in relation to a given subject.

Distinguishing Between Primary and Secondary Sources: The ability to understand the important distinction between sources which are primary (original or eyewitness accounts) and those which are secondary (historically removed from, and based on, primary sources).

Separating Fact from Opinion: The ability to make the basic distinction between factual statements (those which can be demonstrated or verified empirically) and statements of opinion (those which are beliefs or attitudes that cannot be proved).

Distinguishing Between Bias and Reason: The ability to differentiate between statements of prejudice (unfavorable, preconceived judgments based on feelings instead of reason) and

11

statements of reason (conclusions that can be clearly and logically explained or justified).

Identifying Stereotypes: The ability to identify oversimplified, exaggerated descriptions (favorable or unfavorable) about people and insulting statements about racial, religious or national groups, based upon misinformation or lack of information.

Recognizing Ethnocentrism: The ability to recognize attitudes or opinions that express the view that one's own race, culture, or group is inherently superior, or those attitudes that judge another race, culture, or group in terms of one's own.

It is important to consider opposing viewpoints. It is equally important to be able to critically analyze those viewpoints. The activities in this book will give you practice in mastering these thinking skills. Although the activities are helpful to the solitary reader, they are most useful when the reader can benefit from the interaction of group discussion.

Using this book, and others in the series, will help you develop basic reading and thinking skills. These skills should improve your ability to better understand what you read. You should be better able to separate fact from opinion, substance from rhetoric. You should become a better consumer of information in our media-centered culture.

A Values Orientation

Throughout the Opposing Viewpoints Series you are presented conflicting values. A good example is *American Foreign Policy.* The first chapter debates whether foreign policy should be based on the same kind of moral principles that individuals use in guiding their personal actions, or instead be based primarily on doing what best advances national interests, regardless of moral implications.

The series does not advocate a particular set of values. Quite the contrary! The very nature of the series leaves it to you, the reader, to formulate the values orientation that you find most suitable. My purpose, as editor of the series, is to see that this is made possible by offering a wide range of viewpoints which are fairly presented.

David L. Bender
Opposing Viewpoints Series Editor

Introduction

"We know more about war than we do about peace—more about killing than we know about living."

General Omar Bradley, Former US Army Chief of Staff

In August 1910, the month of his death, American philosopher William James published his now famous essay, "The Moral Equivalent of War." In it, he wrote that "war against war is going to be no holiday excursion. The military feelings are too deeply grounded to abdicate their place among our ideals." Events both before and after James's lifetime would seem to justify his somber judgment as they reveal a nearly endless panorama of warfare among members of the human species. From the humble beginnings of recorded history in the farming communities of the ancient Near East to the technological whirlwind we call contemporary civilization, humanity has demonstrated that it is more favorably disposed toward war than toward peace. Indeed, although currently we are living in what may technically be called "peacetime," still there are about forty areas of belligerent activity in the world.

This state of chronic antagonism, which seems to be a permanent part of the human condition, has sparked a centuries-old debate among those devoted to the study of humankind. The debaters have, in large part, fallen into two well-defined categories. On one side, there are those who claim that human aggression results from human nature. In other words, men and women are biologically and psychologically predisposed toward violent behavior. On the other side, there are those who lay the blame on human culture. This group argues that the differing social, political, economic, and religious institutions forged by humankind give rise to the hostilities experienced between peoples and nations.

This anthology of opposing viewpoints explores the question of war and human nature. The materials included are drawn from a wide spectrum of sources in order to lend balance and credibility to the debates. The viewpoints contain, among others, the writings of social, biological, physical, political, and military

13

scientists, theologians, and journalists. Beginning with the nature of human aggression, the subject matter bids the reader to consider why humans engage in hostile activities in which the outcome is often individual or group destruction. And as the reader probes the topics, it might be useful to consider the following: Is this bloody melodrama we call war imprinted indelibly on our genes? Or is it an unnatural condition forced upon us by our institutions, only awaiting some future revelation in an enlightened age before it is eradicated? Today it is not an overstatement to say that our survival as a species is probably totally dependent on the answers to these seminal questions.

CHAPTER 1

Are Humans Aggressive by Nature?

"The sombre fact is that man is the cruellest and most ruthless species that has ever walked the earth."

Aggression Is an Instinct

Anthony Storr

One of the most problematic issues facing social and biological scientists is determining the degree to which human behavior results from environmental or genetic factors. Sometimes referred to as the *Nature* (innate) vs. *Nurture* (learned) debate, countless experiments and studies have been performed in hopes of resolving the issue. Yet the controversy continues to rage unabated. The following viewpoint, by Anthony Storr, focuses upon an area of enormous contention in this debate, namely, the source of human aggression. A prominent English psychiatrist, author, lecturer and radio and television personality, Mr. Storr argues that human aggression is unquestionably grounded in human nature. Indeed, he writes that within every human breast lies "those same savage impulses which lead to murder, to torture and to war."

As you read consider the following questions:

1. Do J. P. Scott and Zing Yan Kuo believe that aggression is an instinct? Explain your answer.
2. In what way does the author compare sex and aggression?
3. How does the author compare his theory to those of Berkowitz and Scott?
4. Do you agree with the author? Why or why not?

That man is an aggressive creature will hardly be disputed. With the exception of certain rodents, no other vertebrate habitually destroys members of his own species. No other animal takes positive pleasure in the exercise of cruelty upon another of his own kind. We generally describe the most repulsive examples of man's cruelty as brutal or bestial, implying by these adjectives that such behaviour is characteristic of less highly developed animals than ourselves. In truth, however, the extremes of 'brutal' behaviour are confined to man; and there is no parallel in nature to our savage treatment of each other. The sombre fact is that we are the cruellest and most ruthless species that has ever walked the earth; and that, although we may recoil in horror when we read in newspaper or history book of the atrocities committed by man upon man, we know in our hearts that each one of us harbours within himself those same savage impulses which lead to murder, to torture and to war. . . .

Is Aggression an Instinct?

Although we cannot give a straightforward and simple answer to the question 'Is aggression an instinct?' what we can say is that, in man, as in other animals, there exists a physiological mechanism which, when stimulated, gives rise both to subjective feelings of anger and also to physical changes which prepare the body for fighting. This mechanism is easily set off, and, like other emotional responses, it is stereotyped and, in this sense, "instinctive." Just as one angry cat is very like another angry cat, so one angry man or woman closely resembles another at the level of physiological response; although, of course, the way in which human beings adapt to and control their feelings of rage differs widely according to training. . . .

The existence of the physiological mechanism is not in doubt. Self-preservation demands that an animal should carry within it the potential for aggressive action, since the natural world is a place in which hostile threats must be overcome or evaded if life is to continue.

Our physiological discussion has shown that the physical mechanism of aggression, aggressive emotions and behavior is indeed 'instinctive' in that it is an inborn, automatic possibility which is easily triggered. But need the trigger be pulled? . . .

Some authors are convinced that there is no essential need for aggressive behavior ever to be manifested. J.M. Scott, in his book *Aggression,* for example, says:

> The important fact is that the chain of causation in every case eventually traces back to the outside. There is no physiologi-

cal evidence of any spontaneous stimulation for fighting aris-
ing within the body. This means that there is no need for
fighting, either aggressive or defensive, apart from what hap-
pens in the external environment. We may conclude that a
person who is fortunate enough to exist in an environment
which is without stimulation to fight will not suffer
physiological or nervous damage because he never fights. This
is a quite different situation from the physiology of eating,
where the internal processes of metabolism lead to definite
physiological changes which eventually produce hunger and

"GOSH! — WHAT MAKES ME SO VIOLENT?"

Reprinted with permission from the *Minneapolis Star and Tribune.*

stimulation to eat, without any change in the external environment.

We can also conclude that there is no such thing as a simple instinct for fighting,' in the sense of an internal driving force which has to be satisfied. There is, however, an internal physiological mechanism which has only to be stimulated to produce fighting. This distinction may not be important in many practical situations, but it leads to a hopeful conclusion regarding the control of aggression. The internal physiological mechanism is dangerous, but it can be kept under control by external means.

Those who are prejudiced in favor of this point of view often quote the experiments of Zing Yang Kuo who discovered that if a kitten was reared in the same cage with a rat it would accept the rat as a campanion and could never afterwards be induced to pursue or kill rats. Kuo concluded that 'The behavior of an organism is a *passive affair*. How an animal or man will behave in a given moment depends on how it has been brought up and how it is stimulated.' . . .

The conclusions of Scott and Kuo that aggression is learned, rather than an expression of an innate drive are not supported by these experiments. The fact that the aggressive response requires an outside stimulus to elicit it does not imply that the organism may not need to behave aggressively or obtain satisfaction from so doing.

Sex and Aggression

It is true that aggressive tension cannot yet be portrayed in physiological terms as we might describe hunger; that is, as a state of deprivation which drives the animal to take action to relieve it. But the same is actually true of the sexual instinct; and most people, rightly or wrongly, accept the idea that sex is 'an internal driving force which has to be satisfied.' The full release of sexual tension is generally thought to require a partner, although a modicum of satisfaction can be obtained by masturbation. In other words, just as with aggression, there is an internal physiological mechanism which needs an outside stimulus to fire it off. Although we generally think of sex as driving an animal to seek the stimulus which will bring internal satisfaction, we do not generally think of aggression in the same terms. Yet we cannot define the sense of tension or deprivation which leads to sexual behavior any more than we can define the possible physiological state which might lead to an animal 'spoiling for a fight' or, at least, needing to make the violent physical efforts for which the body is prepared when the aggressive mechanism is fired. . . .

It is fashionable for academic psychologists to deride the possibility that man's aggression is an endogenous, instinctive impulse which seeks discharge. Although such writers of course admit that man is an aggressive being, they try to explain all human aggression in terms either of a response to frustration, or else as a learned activity, which, because it is rewarded in terms of possessions, praise or status, is constantly reinforced in human societies as they are at present constituted. Thus Leonard Berkowitz, for example, summarizing 'Instinct Concep-

---

This Is Rubbish

Optimism is expressed by some who feel that since we have evolved a high level of intelligence and a strong inventive urge, we shall be able to twist any situation to our advantage; that we are so flexible that we can re-mould our way of life to fit any of the new demands made by our rapidly rising species-status; that when the time comes, we shall manage to cope with the over-crowding, the stress, the loss of our privacy and independence of action; that we shall re-model our behaviour patterns and live like giant ants; that we shall control our aggressive and territorial feelings, our sexual impulses and our parental tendencies; that if we have to become battery-chicken apes, we can do it; that our intelligence can dominate all our basic biological urges. I submit that this is rubbish.

Desmond Morris, *The Naked Ape.*

---

tions of Aggression' writes as follows:

Since 'spontaneous' animal aggression is a relatively rare occurrence in nature (and there is the possibility that even these infrequent cases may be accounted for by frustrations or prior learning of the utility of hostile behavior), many ethologists and experimental biologists rule out the possibility of a self-stimulating aggressive system in animals. One important lesson to be derived from these studies is that there is no instinctive drive toward war within man. Theoretically, at least, it is possible to lessen the likelihood of interpersonal conflict by descreasing the occurrence of frustrations and minimizing the gains to be won through aggression.

Such a point of view can only be sustained if a vast amount of evidence from ethological and anthropological studies is neglected; and must surely rest upon the belief or hope that, if only society were better organized or children reared in ways which did not encourage them to be aggressive, men would live in peace with one another, and the millennium would at least be realized. Such beliefs are as old as history. . .It is, however, particularly characteristic of modern Americans to hold these opinions, since perennial optimism makes it hard for them to believe that there is anything unpleasant either in the physical world or in human nature which cannot be 'fixed.'

We Are Aggressive

Authors such as Berkowitz and Scott never suggest that the sexual impulse could be abolished or seriously modified by learning or by decreasing the rewards of sexual satisfaction, for, in their minds, sex carries a positive sign, whereas aggression is negatively labelled. Yet, it is probable that when no outside stimulus for aggression exists, men actually seek such stimuli out in much the same way as they do when sexually deprived. At the introspective level, it may be true to say that one deplores getting angry; but the physiological changes which accompany anger give rise to a subjective sense of well-being and of invigorating purpose which in itself is rewarding. Appalling barbarities have been justified in the name of 'righteous wrath;' but there can be no doubt that men enjoy the enlivening effect of being angry when they can justify it, and that they seek out opponents whom they can attack. . . .

What we still need to know, and what we may hope that physiologists may soon tell us, is the biochemical state underlying tension, whether this be aggressive or sexual. There must be physiological differences between the animal who is in a state of sexual deprivation and the animal who is spoiling for a fight. But there is so far no convincing evidence that the aggressive response is, at a physiological level, any less instinctive than the sexual response; and, provided that the term aggression is not restricted to actual fighting, aggressive expression may be as necessary a part of being a human being as sexual expression.

*"Man is not programmed to kill
and make war."*

Aggression Is Not
an Instinct

Richard E. Leakey

Richard E. Leakey is at the forefront of that group of social scientists who believe that aggression is not an instinctive human attribute. The son of the late Louis Leakey, the eminent anthropologist, he is a noted, worldwide lecturer and author on the subject of human origins and behavior. The following viewpoint is excerpted from Mr. Leakey's latest book, *The Making of Mankind*. In it, he attempts to explain why he feels that men and women are not the "killer-apes" many social and biological scientists have portrayed them to be.

As you read, consider the following questions:

1. According to the author, with what instincts are humans born?
2. According to the author, how is human culture related to human behavior?
3. Why does the author feel that it is dangerous to believe that humans are innately aggressive?
4. Do you agree with the author? Why or why not?

Running through the history of human evolution is a persistent theme, that is, the elaboration of material and social culture. Most animals interact with the world on the basis of instinctive behaviours, modified to some extent by their own experience, but, as David Pilbeam emphasizes, 'Man is a learning animal *par excellence.* We have more to learn, take longer to do it, learn it in a more complex and yet more efficient way (that is, culturally), and have a unique type of communication system, vocal language, to promote our learning.' Humans come into this world equipped with very few instinctive responses: suckling, crying, smiling and walking may well be the only things human beings do instinctively. What a person eventually becomes, in terms of both behaviour and beliefs, depends on the culture in which that individual is immersed.

Man not only makes culture, but is also made by culture. David Pilbeam explains: 'Whether we have one or two spouses, wear black or white to a funeral, live in societies that have kings or lack chiefs entirely is a function not of our genes but of learning.' Clifford Geertz has stated the relationship between humans and culture thus: 'Without men, no culture, certainly; but equally, and more significantly, without culture, no men.' We come into the world with the potential to lead any one of a thousand lifestyles. But we lead one that is shaped by the cultural traditions into which we were born.

Human Flexibility

The endless variations of cultural styles of dress and language testify to our extreme flexibility. There are no universal rules which people throughout the world obey. Even the prohibitions on murder and incest, though found in most societies, can be broken in some. *Homo sapiens sapiens* is unquestionably the product of natural selection, but the principal characteristic of our behaviour is that it is moulded by the society in which we live.

Against this background it is ludicrous to argue that organized warfare is equivalent to the baboon's aggressive baring of its canine teeth. National leaders who engineer military conflict with another nation are engaged not in aggression but in politics, and the individuals on the battlefields are more like sheep than wolves. Hand-to-hand killing is no doubt carried out in an atmosphere charged with emotion and anger, but think how much indoctrination and depersonalization has been performed in order to bring combatants to this state of mind.

Speaking from the perspective of a prehistorian, Bernard

Campbell has this to say: 'Anthropology teaches us clearly that Man lived at one with nature until, with the beginnings of agriculture, he began to tamper with the ecosystem: an expansion of his population followed. It was not until the development of the temple towns (around 5000 BC) that we find evidence of inflicted death and warfare. This is too recent an event to have had any influence on the evolution of human nature. . . .Man is not programmed to kill and make war, nor even to hunt: his ability to do so is learned from his elders and his peers when his society demands it.' It seems ironic that the capacity for culture, which is shared equally by all the peoples of the world, should be the instrument which also erects barriers between people. Different religious beliefs and ideologies have many times in history been the cause of hatred and conflict.

The Effect of Language

Most ironic of all, however, is the divisive effect of language. No other creature has the human capacity for spoken language, and it is the foundation on which culture is built. Without language, complex social systems and sophisticated technology

---

Love Not War

We do indeed have capabilities of destructiveness, but we also have propensities to cooperation and love; and it is within our capacities as individuals and as a species to choose.

We can cooperate with one another more or less successfully. We may have to learn how all over again now that war is no longer profitable to anyone.

Andrew M. Greeley, *St. Paul Pioneer Press*, October 29, 1978.

---

would be impossible. It is a capacity that brings people together, but it also divides different groups of people through its principal artifact, culture, and because the great diversity of human languages erects barriers to communication between groups.

I believe that the nature of man is more complex than is usually supposed. We do not carry with us the burden of a more primitive and savage past: humans are not 'killer-apes' as has been suggested. Nor are we innately peaceable creatures. Natural selection has endowed us with a behavioural flexibility which is quite unknown in the animal world. Without doubt we are highly social creatures, and in the absence of other individuals with which to interact we would not be human. For several million years our forebears pursued a way of life, hunting-and-gathering, that demanded a degree of co-operation not displayed by other primates. But it would be as wrong to assert that humans are innately co-operative as it would be to say that we are innately aggressive. We are not innately *anything*. Humans are cultural animals, and each one of us is the product of our own particular cultural environment.

Those who believe that man is innately aggressive are providing a convenient excuse for violence and organized warfare. Still worse, such beliefs increase the likelihood that the holocaust which is predicted will indeed come to pass. It is of little consequence how we envisage the nature of the physical universe: the planets continue in their orbits around the sun whether we believe in them or not. But, as psychiatrist Leon Eisenberg stresses, 'The behaviour of men is not independent of the theories of human nature that men adopt.' When, for instance, the nature of mental illness was thought to be marked with violence, 'patients' were chained, beaten and locked up. They reacted with violent fits of rage, thus fulfilling society's image of them. If we allow ourselves to believe that humans are innately aggressive and that we are inevitably driven towards conflict, then nothing is more certain than the eventual fulfillment of that belief.

"Man is a predator whose natural instinct is to kill with a weapon."

Inheritance Influences Human Behavior

Robert Ardrey

African Genesis is one of the most controversial books published on the subject of human behavior in the last thirty years. Labeled "fascinating . . . provocative . . . sensational" by the Saturday Review Syndicate, *African Genesis* is essentially an investigation into the animal origins and nature of man. Its author, Robert Ardrey, was born in Chicago where he majored in natural sciences at the University of Chicago. A successful playwright and screen writer, in 1955, he began his African travels and studies with *African Genesis* being the result of these pursuits. The following viewpoint is excerpted from this book. In it, Mr. Ardrey suggests, in a symbolic way, that all the generations of humanity were spawned by Cain, son of Adam and Eve and murderer of his brother Abel.

As you read, consider the following questions:

1. According to the author, what is the significance of man's enlarging brain?
2. According to the author, what demands do a primate's territorial instincts place upon the primate itself?
3. Why does the author believe that becoming carnivorous was such an important event for man?

What are the things that we know about man? How much have the natural sciences brought to us, so far, in the course of a silent, unfinished revolution? What has been added to our comprehension of ourselves that can support us in our staggering, lighten our burdens in our carrying, add to our hopes, subtract from our anxieties, and direct us through hazard and fog and predicament? Or should the natural sciences have stayed in bed?

We know above all that man is a portion of the natural world and that much of the human reality lies hidden in times past. We are an iceberg floating like a gleaming jewel down the cold blue waters of the Denmark Strait; most of our presence is submerged in the sea. We are a moonlit temple in a Guatemala jungle; our foundations are the secret of darkness and old creepers. We are a thriving, scrambling, elbowing city; but no one can find his way through our labyrinthine streets without awareness of the cities that have stood here before. And so for the moment let us excavate man.

What stands above the surface? His mind, I suppose. The mind is the city whose streets we get lost in, the most recent construction on a very old site. After seventy million years of most gradual primate enlargement, the brain nearly trebled in size in a very few hundreds of thousands of years. Our city is spacious and not lacking in magnificence, but it has the problems of any boom town. Let us dig.

The Children of Cain

We are Cain's children. The union of the enlarging brain and the carnivorous way produced man as a genetic possibility. The tightly packed weapons of the predator form the highest, final, and most immediate foundation on which we stand. . . .

Man is a predator whose natural instinct is to kill with a weapon. The sudden addition of the enlarged brain to the equipment of an armed already-successful predatory animal created not only the human being but also the human predicament. But the final foundation on which we stand has a strange cement. . . .

Let us dig deeper. Layer upon layer of primate preparation lies buried beneath the predatory foundation. As the addition of a suddenly enlarged brain to the way of the hunting primate multiplied both the problems and the promises of the sum total, man, so the addition of carnivorous demands to the non-aggressive, vegetarian primate way multiplied the problems and promises of the sum total, our ancestral hunting primate. . . .

27

The primate has instincts demanding the maintenance and defense of territories; an attitude of perpetual hostility for the territorial neighbour; the formation of social bands as the principal means of survival for a physically vulnerable creature; an attitude of amity and loyalty for the social partner; and varying but universal systems of dominance to insure the efficiency of his social instrument and to promote the natural selection of the more fit from the less. Upon this deeply-buried, complex, primate instinctual bundle were added the necessities and the opportunities of the hunting life. . . .

We can only presume that when the necessities of the hunting life encountered the basic primate instincts, then all were intensified. Conflicts became lethal, territorial arguments minor wars. The social band as a hunting and defensive unit became harsher in its codes whether of amity or enmity. The dominant became more dominant, the subordinate more disciplined. Overshadowing all other qualitative changes, however, was the coming of the aggressive imperative. The creature who had once killed only through circumstance killed now for a living.

The First Cannibals

There is evidence that the first inventors of pebble tools, the African Australopithecines, promptly used their new weapon to kill not only game, but fellow members of their species as well. Peking Man, the Prometheus who learned to preserve fire, used it to roast his brothers: beside the first traces of the regular use of fire lie the mutilated and roasted bones of Sinanthropus pekinensis himself.

Konrad Lorenz, *On Aggression.*

As we glimpsed in the predatory foundation of man's nature. . . so we may see in the coming of the carnivorous way something new and immense and perhaps more significant than the killing necessity. The hunting primate was free. He was free of the forest prison; wherever game roamed the world was his. His hands were freed from the earth or the bough; erect carriage opened new and unguessed opportunities for manual answers to ancient quadruped problems. His daily life was freed from the eternal munching; the capacity to digest high-calorie food meant a life more diverse than one endless meal-time. And his wits were freed. Behind him lay the forest orthodoxies. Ahead of him lay freedom of choice and invention as a new imperative if a revolutionary creature were to meet the unpredictable challenges of a revolutionary way of life. Freedom — as the human being means freedom — was the first gift of the predatory way.

A Powerful Instinct

We may excavate man deeply and ever more deeply as we dig down through pre-primate, pre-mammal, and even pre-land-life levels of experience. We shall pass through the beginnings of sexual activity as a year-around affair, and the consequent beginnings of the primate family. But all the other instincts will be there still deeper down: the instinct to dominate one's fellows, to defend what one deems one's own, to form societies, to mate, to eat and avoid being eaten. The record will grow dim and the outlines blurred. But even in the earliest deposits of our nature where death and the individual have their start, we shall still find traces of animal nostalgia, of fear and dominance and order.

Here is our heritage, so far as we know it today. Here is the excavated mound of our nature with *Homo sapiens'* boom town on top. But whatever tall towers reason may fling against the storms and the promises of the human future, their foundations must rest on the beds of our past for there is nowhere else to build.

Cain's children have their problems. It is difficult to describe the invention of the radiant weapon as anything but the con-

Reprinted with permission from the *Minneapolis Star and Tribune.*

29

summation of a species. Our history reveals the development and contest of superior weapons as *Homo sapiens'* single, universal cultural preoccupation. Peoples may perish, nations dwindle, empires fall; one civilization may surrender its memories to another civilization's sands. But mankind as a whole, with an instinct as true as a meadow-lark's song, has never in a single instance allowed local failure to impede the progress of the weapon, its most significant cultural endowment.

"No human being has ever been born with aggressive or hostile impulses."

Learning Influences Human Behavior

Ashley Montagu

Ashley Montagu is one of the twentieth century's most famous and respected anthropologists. Born in London, England (1905), he immigrated to the United States where he received his Ph.D. in 1937 from Columbia University. During his long and distinguished career, Mr. Montagu has written over three dozen books, many of which deal with both the biological and cultural origins of human behavior. Regarding the nature/nurture controversy, he is an ardent and vocal defender of the hypothesis that human behavior is overwhelmingly influenced by culture and environment. In the following viewpoint, he outlines this position.

As you read, consider the following questions:

1. Why does the author believe that Freud is wrong about men being "savage beasts?"
2. In what way does the author feel that humans differ from animals?
3. Do you agree with the author's arguments? Why or why not?

Ashley Montagu, *The Nature of Human Aggression*. New York: Oxford University Press, copyright 1976. Reprinted with permission of the author.

The writings of the innate aggressionists leave one with the impression that man is little more than a mechanism driven by innate instincts ineradicably inherited from ancestral "killer" apes. . . .

We think the evidence overwhelmingly indicates that it is the social environments of humans that largely determine how their genes, whatever their propensities may be, will express themselves. . . There is good reason to believe that during almost the whole of man's evolutionary history he lived in peace and cooperation with his fellow man. . . .

Freud, in *Civilization and Its Discontents (1930)*, spoke of men as wolves to their fellow men, whose aggressiveness "manifests itself spontaneously and reveals men as savage beasts to whom the thought of sparing their own kind is alien." On every point — on his Hobbesian view of nature, on wolves, on the spontaneity of aggression, on savages, and on beasts — Freud is wrong, profoundly and abysmally wrong. There is no warfare of nature. If there is a law of nature, it is in the balance between cooperation and conflict leading to stable cooperative societies. But in an Age of Conflict this is not the viewing glass through which nature is likely to be looked at. The social context from which we judge events, our particular and special ideologies, color our judgments. Animals make no war, nor are they in a constant state of conflict; rarely do they kill their own kind. In fact, compared with man most animals are natural pacifists. When they fight among themselves seldom is it to inflict injury, and rarely do their fights end in death. Their aggressive behavior is primarily a way of competition rather than destruction. Wolves, contrary to Freud and popular belief, do not attack other wolves. Aggressiveness in men and other animals is not spontaneous, but must have some external stimulus before it can be activated. . . .

Genes and Environment

That human beings inherit genes which influence human behavior is a fact. It is also a fact that genes for basic forms of human behavior such as aggression, love, and altruism are the products of a long evolutionary history, and that in any serious examination of the nature of such forms of human behavior the evolutionary history of the species and its relations must be taken into account. In the development of human behavior evolutionary pressures have been at work over a long period of time, but they are evolutionary pressures that have been influenced by a unique social environment, a wholly new zone of

32

adaptation, namely, that of culture.

As a consequence of cultural selective pressures humanity has greatly influenced the genetic substrates of its own behavioral development. This does not mean that humans have been altogether freed from the influences of genes which similarly affect the behavior of other animals, but it does mean that in humans behavior is far less under the direction of genes than is that of other animals. Furthermore, that the educability, lack of fixity, and remarkable flexibility of the human genetic constitution is such that humans are able, as a consequence of their socialization, to canalize the behavioral expression of genetic influences in all sorts of ways, creative as well as destructive.

Notions Must Change

Nothing could more effectively prolong man's fighting behavior than a belief that aggression is in our genes. An unwelcome cultural inheritance can be eradicated fairly quickly and easily, but the incentive to do it is lacking while people believe that aggression is innate and instinctive with us.

Sally Carrighar, *The New York Times Magazine*, September 10, 1967.

To a greater or lesser extent learning and what is learned are genetically influenced, but learning and what is learned are also influenced to a very large extent by the human environment. To repeat once more, to some extent behavior is always the expression of the interaction between genetic tendencies and environmental influences.

The behavioral species trait of *Homo sapiens*, namely, educability, makes it possible for human beings to mold genetic behavior tendencies in a variety of different ways. Since the expression of genes is a function of the environment, genes are subject to human control. In humans that control can be considerable. Humans differ behaviorally from other animals in their possession of a genetic constitution which is much more amenable to the influences of the cultural environment. This does not, of course, mean that genetic substrates for behavior play an insignificant role in influencing certain human behaviors, but it does mean that such genetic factors do not determine the development of such behaviors.

What we can legitimately conclude when the full range of human behavior is considered, from the most loving to the most murderous, is that humans are creatures potentially capable of

33

any form of behavior, depending largely upon the socialization, the conditioning, which they have undergone from infancy. This is not to deny in any way that some genetic contribution, direct or indirect, is involved in virtually every form of human behavior. But what it does deny is that that behavior is genetically determined. The conditioning environment interacts with the genetic potentials and the resulting behavior is the expression of that interaction. . . .

Potentialities and Educability

Humans are neither naked apes nor fallen angels driven by that original sin, that great power of blackness, which Calvinistic commentators and their modern compeers have declared to actuate us. Neither are humans reducible to the category of animals, for we are the *human* animals, a humanity which adds to being a dimension lacking in all other animals, creatures of immense and extraordinary educability, capable of being molded into virtually every and any desired shape and form. Humans are not born *tabulae rasae,* blank tablets, without any predispositions whatever. They are born with many predispositions, to talk, to think, to engage in sexual behavior, to love, to be aggressive, and the like, but they will achieve none of these behaviors unless they are exposed to the external stimuli necessary for the development of those potentialities into abilities. It takes many months to learn how to speak. It may take years to learn how to love or how to engage in sexual behavior. It may take much less time to learn to be aggressive. . . .

No human being has ever been born with aggressive or hostile impulses, and no one becomes aggressive or hostile without learning to do so. Again, this does not for a moment deny the existence of potentialities for aggression and hostility based on neural arrangements which can be readily organized to function in aggressive behavior. What is denied is that without the added stimulation of those neural arrangements by the appropriate stimuli and their social organization into certain patterns of behavior, aggression will not spontaneously make its appearance in any human being.

The explanation of aggressive human behavior is by no means as simple as the innate aggressionists have made it out to be. It is very much more complex than is suggested by their simplistic and erroneous animal hydraulic models. Simple solutions have an immediate appeal to those who are looking for ready answers to complex problems, but truth is not advanced by explanations

34

based on false analogies with animal behavior, wild extrapolations from animals to human beings, misinterpretations of the evidence both in animals and in humans, neglect of the vitally important verifiable facts of behavior in living non-aggressive human societies, loose speculations and violent distortions of the evidence relating to prehistoric humans, and the attribution to them of traits as genetically determined which are, in fact, for the most part culturally determined.

"Men are . . . . creatures among whose instinctual endowments is to be reckoned a powerful share of aggressiveness."

Humans Are Born Violent

Sigmund Freud

The name of Sigmund Freud (1856-1939) is virtually synonymous with the subject of human behavior. An Austrian psychiatrist, Freud's theories laid the foundation for nearly all modern schools of psychoanalysis. Relatively early in his career, Freud became convinced that humans are born with certain behavioral traits, some of which are potentially destructive to both the individual and society. Aggressiveness is one such trait. In his *Civilization and Its Discontents*, Freud makes the claim that the instinctive life of man is one of aggression and self-satisfaction. The following viewpoint, an excerpt from that work, demonstrates Freud's almost despairing view of the human animal.

As you read, consider the following questions:

1. What examples does Freud offer to support his belief that "man is a savage beast?
2. Does the author believe that civilization has succeeded in containing man's aggressive impulses?
3. Why does Freud claim that the beliefs upon which communism are built will not eliminate aggressive behavior among humans?

Men are not gentle creatures who want to be loved, and who at the most can defend themselves if they are attacked; they are, on the contrary, creatures among whose instinctual endowments is to be reckoned a powerful share of aggressiveness. As a result, their neighbour is for them not only a potential helper or sexual object, but also someone who tempts them to satisfy their aggressiveness on him, to exploit his capacity for work without compensation, to use him sexually without his consent, to seize his possessions, to humiliate him, to cause him pain, to torture and to kill him. Who, in the face of all his experience of life and history, will have the courage to dispute this assertion? As a rule this cruel aggressiveness waits for some provocation or puts itself at the service of some other purpose, whose goal might also have been reached by milder measures. In circumstances that are favourable to it, when the mental counter-forces which ordinarily inhibit it are out of action, it also manifests itself spontaneously and reveals man as a savage beast to whom consideration towards his own kind is something alien. Anyone who calls to mind the atrocities committed during the racial migrations or the invasions of the Huns, or by the people known as Mongols under Jenghiz Khan and Tamerlane, or at the capture of Jerusalem by the pious Crusaders, or even, indeed, the horrors of the recent World War—anyone who calls these things to mind will have to bow humbly before the truth of this view.

The existence of this inclination to aggression, which we can detect in ourselves and justly assume to be present in others, is the factor which disturbs our relations with our neighbour and which forces civilization into such a high expenditure [of energy]. In consequence of this primary mutual hostility of human beings, civilized society is perpetually threatened with disintegration. The interest of work in common would not hold it together; instinctual passions are stronger than reasonable interests. Civilization has to use its utmost efforts in order to set limits to man's aggressive instincts and to hold the manifestations of them in check by psychical reaction-formations. Hence, therefore, the use of methods intended to incite people into identifications and aim-inhibited relationships of love, hence the restriction upon sexual life, and hence too the ideal's commandment to love one's neighbour as oneself—a commandment which is really justified by the fact that nothing else runs so strongly counter to the original nature of man. In spite of every effort these endeavours of civilization have not so far achieved very much. It hopes to prevent the crudest excess of brutal violence by itself assuming the right to use violence against criminals, but the law is not able to lay hold of the more cautious and refined manifestations of human aggressiveness. The time comes when each one of us has to give up as illusions the expectations which, in his youth, he pinned upon his fellow-men, and when he may learn how much difficulty and pain has been added to his life by their ill-will. At the same time, it would be unfair to reproach civilization with trying to eliminate strife and competition from human activity. These things are undoubtedly indIspensable. But opposition is not necessarily enmity; it is merely misused and made an *occasion* for enmity.

The Causes of War

In the nature of man we find three principal causes of quarrel: first, competition; secondly, diffidence; thirdly, glory.

The first makes men invade for gain, the second for safety, and the third for reputation. The first use violence to make themselves masters of other men's persons, wives, children, and cattle; the second, to defend them; the third, for trifles, as a word, a smile, a different opinion, and any other sign of undervalue, either direct in their persons or by reflection in their kindred, their friends, their nation, their profession, or their name.

Hereby it is manifest that, during the time men live without a common power to keep them all in awe, they are in that condition which is called war, and such a war as is of every man against every man.

Thomas Hobbes, *Leviathan.*

Communism and Private Property

The communists believe that they have found the path to deliverance from our evils. According to them, man is wholly good and is well-disposed to his neighbour; but the institution of private property has corrupted his nature. The ownership of private wealth gives the individual power, and with it the temptation to ill-treat his neighbour; while the man who is excluded from possession is bound to rebel in hostility against his oppressor. If private property were abolished, all wealth held in common, and everyone allowed to share in the enjoyment of it, ill-will and hostility would disappear among men. Since everyone's needs would be satisfied, no one would have any reason to regard another as his enemy; all would willingly undertake the work that was necessary. I have no concern with

38

any economic criticisms of the communist system; I cannot enquire into whether the abolition of private property is expedient or advantageous. But I am able to recognize that the psychological premises on which the system is based are an untenable illusion. In abolishing private property we deprive the human love of aggression of one of its instruments, certainly a strong one, though certainly not the strongest; but we have in no way altered the differences in power and influence which are misused by aggressiveness, nor have we altered anything in its nature. Aggressiveness was not created by property. It reigned almost without limit in primitive times, when property was still very scanty, and it already shows itself in the nursery almost

'Just between ourselves, your obsession that the rest of society is mad is probably true ... but they are in charge'

Norris – Vancouver Sun/Rothco.

before property has given up its primal, anal form; it forms the basis of every relation of affection and love among people. If we do away with personal rights over material wealth, there still remains prerogative in the field of sexual relationships, which is bound to become the source of the strongest dislike and the most violent hostility among men who in other respects are on an equal footing. If we were to remove this factor, too, by allowing complete freedom of sexual life and thus abolishing the family, the germ-cell of civilization, we cannot, it is true, easily foresee what new paths the development of civilization could take; but one thing we can expect, and that is that this indestructible feature of human nature will follow it there.

It is clearly not easy for men to give up the satisfaction of this inclination to aggression. They do not feel comfortable without it. The advantage which a comparatively small cultural group offers of allowing this instinct an outlet in the form of hostility against intruders is not to be despised. It is always possible to bind together a considerable number of people in love, so long as there are other people left over to receive the manifestations of their aggressiveness.

"Man's propensity for violence is not a racial or a species attribute woven in his genetic fabric."

Culture Has Generated Violence

Rene Dubos

In his anthology, *Man and Aggression,* Ashley Montagu offers a broad selection of essays by social and biological scientists who attempt to show that man is the product of his environment. The following viewpoint, by the late Rene Dubos, a former bacteriologist at The Rockefeller University, is taken from that anthology and first appeared in *The American Scholar.* In it, Mr. Dubos explains that human social institutions, not human genes, are largely responsible for man's seeming propensity toward violence.

As you read, consider the following questions:

1. What are the opinions the author offers about the origins of human aggression?
2. What conclusions does the author draw from his experiments with laboratory animals?
3. What explanation does the author offer for man becoming a killer of his own species?

Reprinted from THE AMERICAN SCHOLAR, Volume 40, Number 4, Autumn, 1971. Copyright © by the United Chapters of Phi Beta Kappa. By permission of the publishers.

The events of recent years seem indeed to prove that one of mankind's chief occupations is destructive warfare and other forms of violence—deliberately practiced. Men have consciously tortured and killed their fellowmen in Algeria, Vietnam, Biafra, the Middle East, in city streets all over the world and even on college campuses. Destructive violence is as much a part of life today as it was in Homer's time.

Revulsion against violence, however, is also one of the hallmarks of human history. The soul-searching and protests generated by the tragedies of the past few years are almost as impressive as the tragedies themselves. In every part of the world, furthermore, there are countless normal human beings who would find it extremely painful, if not emotionally impossible, to kill another human being or even to exhibit aggressive behavior. It takes a great deal of conditioning to prepare a nation for war, and to train soldiers to kill by hand-to-hand combat. While it is obvious that many men are killers, it is equally true that many are not. And for this reason it seems hardly justified to state that Man—with a capital M—is by nature a killer.

One need not be an anthropologist or a historian to know that violence and conflict have existed in all human societies under many different forms, but opinions differ about the origins of human aggression. Some regard it as purely the consequence of cultural or social conditioning. Others believe that it is the direct and inevitable expression of instincts that are indelibly inscribed in man's genetic code. This polarization of views constitutes in reality a pseudo problem, analogous in all respects to the now worn-out nurture *versus* nature controversy. The potentiality for aggressiveness is indeed part of man's genetic constitution, just as it is part of the genetic constitution of all animal species. But the manifestation of all genetic potentialities are shaped by past experiences and present circumstances. There is no genetic coding that inevitably results in aggressiveness, only a set of genetic attributes for self-defense that can become expressed as aggressiveness under particular sets of conditions. . . .

Revealing Experiments

Certain men act as killers under certain conditions because social life often distorts the instinctive responses that are essential for self-defense. The instinct for preservation exists in all animals and can generate violent behavior even in the most timid species. Rabbits and mice are readily frightened under ordinary circumstances, but they can fight just as viciously as tigers, wolves, baboons and men whenever any of their fundamental "values" are involved. I have seen a rabbit repeatedly and ferociously assault a huge black snake threatening its nest. Time and time again in the laboratory, I have observed tame white mice—so gentle that a child could handle them—engage in fierce fighting against mice of the same breed and age introduced into their cage from the outside. Violent conflict among these mice occurred even though food and water were abundant, the animals were not crowded, and they did not have occasion to fight for females. It would be silly to say that Rabbit or Mouse is a killer because rabbits and mice will fight to defend their young or their territory, or against a stranger introduced from the outside. In animals as well as in men, many manifestations of the instinct for self-defense result in aberrant forms of behavior that are destructive rather than biologically useful.

What Determines Me

I certainly believe that my own behavior is entirely a function of three things—my genetic endowment, my past history as an individual (my family, my religious experience, my government, my schooling, the physical environment in which I have lived, and so on), and the present situation. I am absolutely sure that that is all there is in the determination of what I'm going to do at this very moment.

B. F. Skinner, *Psychology Today*, November 1972.

In animal life the instinct of self-preservation evolved to deal through short-term responses with situations apprehended by the senses. In man, the expressions of the same fundamental instinct have usually been translated from the plane of nature to the plane of society, from sensual perceptions to symbolic conceptions, from short-term responses to long-range effects. If man behaves more commonly as a killer than do animals, it is because his ways of life, his social history, and his mental processes often place him in situations that differ radically from those under which he evolved and in which he acquired the instinct for self-defense. Comparative observations of animals living in zoos or in their natural habitats help to explain how social forces can make man behave as a killer through aberrations of his instinctive defense responses.

In captivity as well as in the wild, males compete for territory and for the available females especially during the rut season. The savage fights among stags, walrus bulls and seals are part of the wildlife lore. The combat between males, however, is rarely to the death. The weaker combatant turns aside and retreats; the victor lets the vanquished go unmolested. Among animals under natural conditions and often in captivity, fighting presents some analogy to German student duels; certain types of wounds are permissible but most battles are limited to bluffing contests and to confrontations of wits. Furthermore, fighting between animals of the same species is often symbolic rather than real. Animals tend to ritualize their aggression by such attitudes as rearing up, roaring, showing their teeth, or erecting their ruffs, hackles or neck hair. Ritualization of behavior is widespread among higher apes, and also, of course, among men. . . .

The Human Predicament

When man emerged from his animal background, he created ways of life and environments in which the social restraints achieved during the early phases of his evolution were no longer effective or suitable. Biological adaptation has not prepared him for the competitive attitudes that prevail in most societies. Man becomes a killer of his own species because he has failed to develop social restraints capable of substituting for the biological wisdom evolved under natural conditions. Violence and internecine conflict are most common in highly competitive societies, particularly during periods of rapid change that upset social order. Man has not yet learned to live in the zoos he has created for himself. . . .

To minimize the destructive effects of violence, we might find it profitable humbly to take a lesson from the animal world and try systematically to ritualize our conflicts. War games among primitive people, the jousts of medieval knights, and some of the later gentlemanly conventions of military behavior had in fact some similarities to the sham fights so common among animals, not only in the wild but also in tame populations. If modern societies could develop effective techniques for the ritualization of conflicts—by global Olympic games, for example, or by space exploration—they might achieve something like what William James called the moral equivalent of war. Battles of bravado might go far toward averting the destructive effects of violence.

Man's propensity for violence is not a racial or species attribute woven in his genetic fabric. It is culturally conditioned by history and the ways of life. The instinct for self-defense exists throughout the animal kingdom and can exhibit aberrant manifestations in animals as well as in man—more frequently in man only because he always lives under conditions that differ profoundly from the ones under which he evolved. We cannot escape from the zoos we have created for ourselves and return to wilderness, but we can improve our societies and make them better suited to our unchangeable biological nature.

Distinguishing Between Fact and Opinion

This activity is designed to help develop the basic reading and thinking skill of distinguishing between fact and opinion. Consider the following statement as an example. "Israel has one of the most effective armies in the Middle East." This statement is a fact which no historian, political commentator or diplomat of any nationality would deny. But consider a statement which condemns Israel and its army. "The aggressiveness and imperialistic aims of Israel and its army is the chief cause of tensions in the Middle East." Such a statement is clearly an expressed opinion. The motives attributed to Israeli military policy as carried out by the army of Israel obviously will depend upon one's point of view. A citizen of Israel will view the activities of his/her army from a far different perspective than will a member of the Palestine Liberation Organization.

When investigating controversial issues it is important that one be able to distinguish between statements of fact and statements of opinion.

The following statements are taken from the viewpoints in this chapter. Consider each statement carefully. *Mark O for any statement you feel is an opinion or interpretation of facts. Mark F for any statement you believe is a fact.*

If you are doing this activity as a member of a class or group compare your answers with those of other class or group members. Be able to defend your answers. You may discover that others will come to different conclusions than you. Listening to the reasons others present for their answers may give you valuable insights in distinguishing between fact and opinion.

If you are reading this book alone, ask others if they agree with your answers. You too will find this interaction very valuable.

O = opinion
F = fact

46

1. The sombre fact is that human beings are the cruelest and most ruthless species that have ever walked the earth.

2. Self-preservation demands that an animal should carry within it the potential for aggressive action.

3. Aggressive expression may be as necessary a part of being a human being as sexual expression.

4. What a person eventually becomes, in terms of both behavior and beliefs, depends on the culture in which that individual is immersed.

5. No other creature has the human capacity for spoken language.

6. Those who believe that man is innately aggressive are providing a convenient excuse for violence and organized warfare.

7. Man is a predator whose natural instinct is to kill with a weapon.

8. Animals make no war, nor are they in a constant state of conflict.

9. That human beings inherit genes which influence human behavior is a fact.

10. No human being has ever been born with aggressive or hostile impulses.

11. Men are not gentle creatures who want to be loved.

12. In consequence of the mutual hostility of human beings, civilized society is perpetually threatened with disintegration.

13. The events of recent years seem indeed to prove that one of mankind's chief occupations is destructive warfare and other forms of violence.

14. While it is obvious that many men are killers, it is equally true that many more are not.

15. There is no genetic coding that inevitably results in aggressiveness.

16. Violence and mutually destructive conflict are most common in highly competitive societies.

Bibliography

The following list of books deals with the subject matter of this chapter.

Robert Ardrey	*The Territorial Imperative.* New York: Dell Publishing Company, 1966.
Elliot Aronson	*The Social Animal,* San Francisco: W. H. Freeman and Company, 1972.
Ronald H. Bailey	*Violence and Aggression,* New York: Time-Life Books, 1976.
Stephan Chorover	*From Genesis to Genocide: The Meaning of Human Nature and the Power of Behavior Control,* Cambridge: MIT Press, 1980.
Lee Ehrman and Peter Parsons	*Behavior, Genetics and Evolution,* New York: McGraw-Hill, 1981.
Erich Fromm	*The Anatomy of Human Destructiveness,* New York: Holt, Rinehart and Winston, 1973.
Konrad Lorenz	*On Aggression,* New York: Harcourt Brace Jovanovich, 1966.
Ashley Montagu, ed.	*Learning Non-Aggression,* New York: Oxford University Press, 1978.
Ashley Montagu, ed.	*Man and Aggression,* New York: Oxford University Press, 1973.
Desmond Morris	*The Naked Ape,* New York: Dell Publishing Company, 1967.
William McDougall	*Janus: The Conquest of War, a Psychological Enquiry,* New York: Garland Publishing, 1972.
Wilfred T. Russell	*The Role of Violence in History and the Metaphysics of War,* Alberquerque: Institute for Economic and Political World Strategic Studies, 1979.
Harry H. Turney-High	*Primitive War: Its Practice and Concepts,* Columbia: University of South Carolina Press, 1971.
J. Young	*An Introduction to the Study of Man,* New York: Oxford University Press, 1971.

What Causes War?

"In general, those who plan do not kill and those who kill do not plan."

Modern Bureaucracies Cause War

Richard J. Barnet

Richard J. Barnet is a Senior Fellow of the Institute for Policy Studies, an independent center in Washington, D.C. devoted to research on public policy questions. A graduate of Harvard College and Harvard Law School, he was an official of the State Department and the Arms Control and Disarmament Agency and a consultant to the Department of Defense during the Kennedy Administration. Mr. Barnet is a prolific writer whose articles have appeared in major magazines and newspapers across the U.S. He has also authored several books including *Who Wants Disarmament?* (1960), *The Giants: Russia and America* (1977) and the forthcoming *The Alliance: America, Europe, and Japan. A History of the Post-War World.* The following viewpoint is excerpted from his *Roots of War.* In it, he explains the ways in which modern bureaucracies are responsible for the causes and nature of modern warfare.

As you read, consider the following questions:

1. What does the author mean by "bureaucratic homicide"?
2. According to the author, how do 20th century conceptions of war differ from those of earlier times?
3. According to the author, why was the atomic bomb dropped on Hiroshima and Nagasaki?

Thinkers with as different a view of the world as Sigmund Freud and Mikhail Bakunin have been struck by the fact that the role of the state is to assert a monopoly on crime. Individuals get medals, promotions, and honors by committing the same acts for the state for which they would be hanged or imprisoned in any other circumstance. "If we did for ourselves what we did for our country," Cavour once observed, "what rascals we should all be." The very meaning of sovereignty which states guard so jealously is the magical power to decide what is or is not a crime. The "state" is of course an abstraction to describe the activities of thousands of human beings organized into bureaucratic structures.

There is nothing new, to be sure, about government-ordered slaughters. Since man first built cities, from the Assyrians to Genghis Khan, from the Crusades to the Indian Wars, war has been an instrument of policy. No age has escaped the passion and fury of the professional killer. It is not homicide in the line of duty that is new, but the incredibly sophisticated organization of homicidal activities and techniques.

The essential characteristic of bureaucratic homicide is division of labor. In general, those who plan do not kill and those who kill do not plan. The scene is familiar. Men in blue, green, and Khaki tunics and others in three-button business suits sit in pastel offices and plan complex operations in which thousands of distant human beings will die. The men who planned the saturation bombings, free fire zones, defoliation, crop destruction, and assassination programs in the Vietnam War never personally killed anyone.

The bureaucratization of homicide is responsible for the routine character of modern war, the absence of passion, and the efficiency of mass-produced death. . . .

The complexity and vastness of modern bureaucratic government complicates the issue of personal responsibility. At every level of government the classic defense of the bureaucratic killer is available: "I was just doing my job!" The essence of bureaucratic government is emotional coolness, orderliness, implacable momentum, and a dedication to abstract principle. Each cog in the bureaucratic machine does what it is supposed to do. . . .

Twentieth Century Technology

Bureaucratic homicide is the monster child of technology and expansionism. The slow tentative progress human beings have made in the direction of civilization has been overwhelmed by the phenomenal advances in lethal technology. Not many people

51

Richard J. Barnet

today believe with the Prussian militarists of a hundred years ago that war is the health of the state, and fewer dare to say so publicly. Twentieth-century man demonstrates in law and political propaganda a sensitivity to human suffering which did not trouble fifteenth-century man. But the modest advances in civilization have been more than wiped out by technological developments which make it possible to kill without exertion, without passion, and without guilt. The airplane enables the cool contemporary killer to set his victims on fire without ever laying eyes on them. The mass air raid and the repeated air strike which long ago were rationalized as conventional warfare by the prophets of airpower, such as General Billy Mitchell and the Italian General Douhet, make destruction "systematic" in a quite literal sense. Americans, along with Germans and British to a lesser degree, have been engaged in this form of bureaucratic homicide for almost thirty years, since the decision in 1942 to bomb Germany into submission. A milestone was the fire raid on Tokyo in 1944, when fire bombs incinerated one hundred eighty thousand residents of the city. Along with new developments in lethal technology have come new ideologies and organizational structures which offer absolution to honorable men when they plan homicide in behalf of the state.

Bureaucracy by nature finds it easy to accept an assigned homicidal role. On January 20, 1942, Reinhard Heydrich, the chief of the SS, called a meeting of fifteen high-ranking representatives of various ministries to the lovely Berlin suburb of Wannsee "to clear up the fundamental problems" of getting rid of all the Jews of Europe. Plans were carefully and coolly discussed and implemented. Although there was serious discussion of the transportation problems connected with the "final solution," no one questioned the project. Adolph Eichmann was a dispassionate long-range killer who, according to testimony at his trial, hated to visit the camps. His pleasure was in designing virtuoso solutions to complicated logistical problems. The psy-

---

Power Mongers
The craving for power which characterises the governing class in every nation is hostile to any limitation of the national sovereignty. This political power-hunger is wont to batten on the activities of another group, whose aspirations are on purely mercenary, economic lines. I have specially in mind that small but determined group, active in every nation, composed of individuals who, indifferent to social considerations and restraints, regard warfare, the manufacture and sale of arms, simply as an occasion to advance their personal interests and enlarge their personal authority.

Albert Einstein, from a letter to Sigmund Freud, July 30, 1932.

---

chiatrist who visited him in an Israeli jail reported that his tests revealed an "insatiable killing intention," but his record suggests that he would do any job of disposal well. The bureaucratic killer looks at an assigned homicidal task as a technical operation much like any other. He does not question its moral purpose. Indeed, he is not even interested in such questions. . . .

The Atomic Bomb
One important force behind bureaucratic homicide is the technological imperative. This is the classic compulsion of modern organizations to push technology to its limits and to exploit it to its fullest. It is, of course, a metaphor to say that technology

dictates policy, for people, not machines, make the decisions. Yet the universal impulse in contemporary bureaucracies to seek prestige on the "frontier of technology" and to seek solution of human problems through technological devices is a crucial factor in the exponential rise of the global body count. "Having made the bomb," President Truman told the American people in August 1945, as if restating the obvious, "we used it." A committee of distinguished Americans, including the President of Harvard, the President of Massachusetts Institute of Technology, the president of one of the largest insurance companies, a former Supreme Court Justice, and a former Secretary of State recommended unanimously "that the bomb be used against the enemy as soon as it could be done . . . without specific warning and against a target that would clearly show its devastating strength."

The President of Harvard made it clear in the committee meetings that the only target meeting such criteria was a population center. The people of Hiroshima and Nagasaki were about as defenseless against a high flying B-29 with an atomic bomb as the Jews in Hitler's Europe were against the gas chambers and ovens. Harry Truman always took personal responsibility for the decision and defended the bomb as "just another weapon." Although there was substantial evidence at the time that the Japanese were considering surrender, the two bombs were dropped "to save lives." Truman's "decision" to drop the bomb was, more accurately, a decision not to stop a bureaucratic process in which more than $2 billion and four years of incredible effort had been invested. The fact that the United States possessed a second bomb, the "Big Boy," which operated on a different, still untested, scientific principle from the "Fat Man" that destroyed Hiroshima, may well account for the totally indefensible Nagasaki attack. Truman never saw anything incongruous about combining his moral defense of Hiroshima and his moral condemnation of hunting in the same book. (One should not shoot at animals that can't shoot back.)

"It seems quite clear that our cultural evolution is at the root of the trouble."

Human Culture Causes War

N. Tinbergen

One of the more common arguments regarding the cause of war is that war is perpetuated by human culture. Culture may be defined as the customs and civilization of a particular people or group. It is essentially the sum total of the ideas, material objects and institutions of a society. The following viewpoint attempts to illustrate the ways in which culture has contributed to human conflict. Authored by N. Tinbergen, a former professor of animal behavior of the Department of Zoology, University of Oxford, England, it explains why cultural change has made man a "misfit in his own society."

As you read, consider the following questions:

1. According to the author, in what ways has human cultural evolution contributed to human warfare?
2. Do you agree with the author? Why or why not?

"On War and Peace in Animals and Man", Tinbergen, N., *Science* Vol. 160, pp. 1411-1418, 28 June 1968. Copyright 1968 by the American Association for the Advancement of Science.

Man has the ability, unparalleled in scale in the animal kingdom, of passing on his experiences from one generation to the next. By this accumulative and exponentially growing process, which we call cultural evolution, he has been able to change his environment progressively out of all recognition. And this includes the social environment. This new type of evolution proceeds at an incomparably faster pace than genetic evolution. Genetically we have not evolved very strikingly since Cro-Magnon man, but culturally we have changed beyond recognition, and are changing at an ever-increasing rate. It is of course true that we are highly adjustable individually, and so could hope to keep pace with these changes. But I am not alone in believing that this behavioral adjustability, like all types of modifiability, has its limits. These limits are imposed upon us by our hereditary constitution, a constitution which can only change with the far slower speed of genetic evolution. There are good grounds for the conclusion that man's limited behavioral adjustability has been outpaced by the culturally determined changes in his social environment, and that this is why man is not a misfit in his own society.

Culture and Warfare

We can now, at last, return to the problem of war, of uninhibited mass killing. It seems quite clear that our cultural evolution is at the root of the trouble. It is our cultural evolution that has caused the population explosion. In a nutshell, medical science, aiming at the reduction of suffering, has, in doing so, prolonged life for many individuals as well—prolonged it to well beyond the point at which they produce offspring. Unlike the situation in any wild species, recruitment to the human population consistently surpasses losses through mortality. Agricultural and technical know-how have enabled us to grow food and to exploit other natural resources to such an extent that we can still feed (though only just) the enormous numbers of human beings on our crowded planet. The result is that we now live at a far higher density than that in which genetic evolution has molded our species. This, together with long-distance communication, leads to far more frequent, in fact to continuous, intergroup contacts, and so to continuous external provocation of aggression. Yet this alone would not explain our increased tendency to kill each other; it would merely lead to continuous threat behavior.

The upsetting of the balance between aggression and fear (and this is what causes war) is due to at least three other conse-

56

quences of cultural evolution. It is an old cultural phenomenon that warriors are both brainwashed and bullied into all-out fighting. They are brainwashed into believing that fleeing—originally, as we have seen, an adaptive type of behavior—is despicable, "cowardly." This seems to me due to the fact that man, accepting that in moral issues death might be preferable to fleeing, has falsely applied the moral concept of "cowardice" to matters of mere practical importance—to the dividing of living space. The fact that our soldiers are also bullied into all-out fighting (by penalizing fleeing in battle) is too well known to deserve elaboration.

Instruments of Warfare

Another cultural excess is our ability to make and use killing tools, especially long-range weapons. These make killing easy, not only because a spear or a club inflicts, with the same effort,

---

What Culture Brings

The emergence of culture has brought no end to the struggle. On the contrary, in cultured societies violence has been organized into wars, wars that may embroil the whole world. Kant writes: "Peace among men living side by side is not a natural state; natural to them is rather a state of war, if not always open hostilities at least the eternal threat of them." The frequency of outbreak has remained more or less the same over the millennia; no tendency to diminish is to be perceived. On the contrary, it might be maintained that the present century is more restless than others in this respect. War is a permanent feature of our life, surviving from one historical period to another regardless of all change in social and political systems, in religions, ethics, intellectual and technical standards. These systems have simply altered the nature of war

Urpo Harva, *War and Human Nature.*

---

so much more damage than a fist, but also, and mainly, because the use of long-range weapons prevents the victim from reaching his attacker with his appeasement, reassurance, and distress signals. Very few aircrews who are willing, indeed eager, to drop their bombs "on target" would be willing to strangle, stab, or burn children (or, for that matter, adults) with their own hands; they would stop short of killing, in response to the appeasement and distress signals of their opponents.

These three factors alone would be sufficient to explain how we have become such unhinged killers. But I have to stress once more that all this, however convincing it may seem, must still be studied more thoroughly.

There is a frightening, and ironical paradox in this conclusion: that the human brain, the finest life-preserving device created by evolution, has made our species so successful in mastering the outside world that it suddenly finds itself taken off guard. One could say that our cortex and our brainstem (our "reason" and our "instincts") are at loggerheads. Together they have created a new social environment in which, rather than ensuring our survival, they are about to do the opposite. The brain finds itself seriously threatened by an enemy of its own making. It is its own enemy. We simply have to understand this enemy.

"We crave scapegoats, targets to absorb our self-doubts, our feelings of worthlessness and hopelessness."

The Need for Scapegoats Causes War

Robert Coles

The following viewpoint offers a somewhat unique explanation as to the cause of war. It was written by Robert Coles, professor of psychiatry and medical humanities at Harvard Medical School and author of the five-volume *Children of Crisis*. Anecdotal in nature, the viewpoint attributes human conflict to a particular quirk in the human condition, namely, people's need to find scapegoats. In essence, Mr. Coles claims that individual and group inadequacies, rather than remaining internalized, are redirected, in a hostile way, toward those outside the group. The result is conflict which, at times, leads to widespread warfare.

As you read, consider the following questions:

1. What does the author mean when he writes that "we crave scapegoats"?
2. What examples does the author offer to support his thesis?
3. Do you agree with the author? Why or why not?

Robert Coles, "Psychology and Armageddon", May, 1982. REPRINTED FROM PSYCHOLOGY TODAY MAGAZINE. Copyright © 1982 American Psychological Association.

We know, through theory, through the reflection of important thinkers, about our various psychological drives; about the way social and political forces connect with our everyday lives, including our dreams and fantasies. But by no means do we have enough knowledge of how individuals (and their leaders) manage in the face of the actual conflicts, the racial and religious and national confrontations, the wars that grab our attention on the evening news.

A Pakistani in Ulster

I have in mind, for example, Northern Ireland, where I have been working in recent years. A terrible religious war, of sorts, has plagued that sector of Europe, off and on, for generations. Catholics and Protestants, one is told again and again, are locked into an impasse that seems unbreakable. The more that historians or social scientists have studied the situation, the less encouraging they have been with respect to answers or solutions. Yet here is what a Pakistani man, a soldier in the British Army, stationed in Ulster, told my young son and me in 1979: "These people hate each other; you are right. But they would become brothers overnight if 500 or 1,000 Pakistanis, like me, came to settle in Belfast—brothers under the skin!"

Merely an anecdotal remark, a soldier's grim and wry sense of things. But, in fact, that young man had done his own kind of psychological and sociological research. He had heard the meanness and nastiness of Irish Catholics and Irish Protestants give way, in his case, to a fear or two about "Pakis," and he had conjectured, as did Freud in Group Psychology and the Analysis of the Ego, that people can indeed change, and dramatically, given a new set of social or racial circumstances. We crave scapegoats, targets to absorb our self-doubts, our feelings of worthlessness and hopelessness. The Pakistani soldier knew this: What Protestants and Catholics have been doing for centuries to one another could, in a moment, turn into a racial rather than a religious confrontation. He also knew an oft-repeated truth: "I guess you could bring the whole earth together—no more war!—if there were another planet, and there were people on it, and they were a threat to us, and we looked upon them as our enemies."

To be hopeful, this soldier recognized, at least, that there are possibilities for a larger sense of loyalty and affiliation than seem to exist now; that the nation-state, or skin color, are not the only symbolic rallying grounds for human beings as they try to define who they are and what they believe to be important. I have heard similar observation in South Africa, where a racial deadlock

60

seems all too evidently a permanent aspect of life—and where a violent war seems never too remote a likelihood. A black child from Soweto kept asking me why white people "don't find other people to hate, and leave us [blacks] alone." A colored child from Capetown kept asking why white people "only see us as darker than themselves, but forget that we're lighter than the Zulus." A white child from Pretoria wondered why the Japanese are considered "white" by the South African government, but not the Chinese. The white child's father observed that such a designation for Japanese visitors was merely "honorary"—a response to obvious commercial imperatives, given Japan's extremely strong economic situation. But the child was undaunted: "If we can do it with the Japanese, we can do it with everyone, and then the country will be even richer than it'll be doing business with Japan, because we won't have a war coming, so we'll save a lot of money that way."

How Children Learn

Such a mix of innocence, practicality, and intelligent compassion—in a child whose parents are tough Afrikaners, all too committed to the principles of apartheid. We need to know more about the manner in which children like that one learn their moral and political values—the manner in which nationally sanctioned ideologies become each individual's articles of personal faith. We also need to know about the inconsistencies in the various nationalist slogans and political ideologies that mesmerize so many millions of this earth's people. I have for years heard American children say, in one breath, how kind and generous we must all be with one another, as Christ urged, and as their Sunday school teachers urge, and, in the next breath, talk about the importance of winning at all costs; and if others lose, "then that's the way it is." Similarly in Ulster, or worse because Christ, of all people, is used as a justification for paramilitary wars.

One wonders whether there might not be a positive means by which solidarity can be achieved without a new outcast group.

A Possible Answer

I will never forget an interview I did in 1963 with a member of the Ku Klux Klan. A desperate, hateful man poured out his frustrations and bitterness, his lifelong resentments and failures. His language was full of obscenities and self-revealing (and self-debasing) cries for struggle and social upheaval—as if, then, he would have his much-wanted (and needed) second chance to

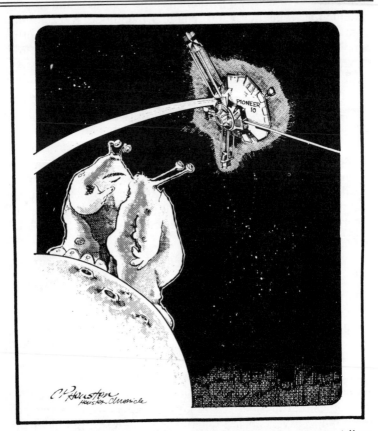

'The enviable thing is that a species that clever must live in a world without war, strife, hunger, disease ...'

C.P. Houston *Houston Chronicle*. Reprinted with permission.

show himself able to make something of himself in the world. He was urging, really, a war—a war of all against all. He was mad, I thought. Yet he was also an ordinary American workingman, having a fairly hard time making a living, and with lots of sickness in his family and little money to meet the growing stack of bills on his kitchen table. I told him, in a moment of exasperation, that he seemed to be arguing the desirability of one more world war; and that I doubted that human life on this planet would survive such an outcome. He looked at me sharply and long; I girded myself for still additional irrationalities, banalities, indecencies. Instead, this: "There's a side of everyone that's mean as can be. There's another side that's good, like my 7-year-old daughter can be, most of the time. What makes the difference is how you live. If you've got a lousy life, the meanness wins. If you've got things pretty good, you have a better chance of being nice to others. The same goes with countries. When a country is in bad shape, its people turn sour, and vice versa. We'll always have wars, where you have a lot of people not having their next meal to take for granted. If the people with lots gave to the people with little, there might be less trouble between countries."

A beginning, that, in thinking about wars. A beginning agenda for psychologists, as well — to try to comprehend how such sentiments, often present and unrecognized in even the most truculent of people, might become harnessed to a given nation's, a given continent's, a given world's social policies.

"Sheer hunger has driven men into battle much more often than people brought up in opulent countries can imagine."

Limited Resources Causes War

Stanislav Andreski

Deprivation has often been cited as a cause of conflict between individuals, groups and nations. As human resources dwindle, human desperation experiences a proportionate increase. The following viewpoint, by Stanislav Andreski, supports this thesis. Formerly of the Department of Sociology, University of Reading, England, Mr. Andreski suggests that more wars have originated from human want than from any other cause. He concludes by noting that if wars are to cease permanently, so must poverty.

As you read, consider the following questions:

1. Does the author believe that world government can bring about universal peace? Why or why not?
2. According to the author, what are the three motives for which people support aggression?
3. What is Malthus's theory on food and population?
4. What is the author's explanation for the origin of war?

Stanislav Andreski, "Origins of War". From *The Natural History of Aggression*, J.D. Carthy and F.J. Ebling, eds. *Institute of Biology Synposia* No. 13. Reprinted with permission. Copyright 1964 by Academic Press, Inc. (London) Ltd.

There are inexhaustible records narrating the origins of particular wars, but war as a pattern of activity antedates by far the art of writing, and therefore the problem of its origins in the strict sense is insoluble. At most we can consider what might be the causes of its ubiquity. . . .

War has been blamed on human nature, and it is perfectly true that if all men were kind and wise there would be no wars. It is clear that the capacity for cruelty is required for war, and the proneness to collective follies always facilitates wars and other kinds of social conflicts. Fortunately, however, there are reasons for doubting whether war is an absolutely necessary consequence of human nature being what it is. . . .

No Innate Tendency

If men had an innate propensity towards war, similar to their desire for food or sexual satisfaction, then there could be no instance of numerous nations remaining at peace for more than a generation. Nor can war be regarded as an inevitable consequence of national sovereignty because there are examples of sovereign states which have waged no wars for more than a century—these are Switzerland, Sweden, Norway and Denmark. One could say that with Switzerland, surrounded as it is by much more powerful neighbours—peacefulness is a matter of necessity rather than choice, but as far as the Scandinavian countries are concerned, it is clear that although they were too weak to attack their neighbours to the south, they could have fought among themselves, as many other small states did. . .

It is often claimed that the remedy against war is to institute a world government but this view can be easily refuted. In the first place, political unification often merely means that instead of interstate wars, civil wars take place which can be just as bad or even worse. To mention one of very many possible examples: as soon as the Romans defeated their dangerous enemies, they started fighting among themselves, thus bringing the lands which they "pacified" into a much worse condition than they were in when they were divided into a multitude of independent and warring states. During the last hundred years the countries which waged fewest wars—Spain, Portugal and the republics of Latin America—had the longest record of internecine strife and revolutions. . . .

The Work of Despots

It must be remembered that wars against rebels constituted, next to external wars, the chief occupation of governments throughout history. On the other hand, the only really peaceful area of the world—Scandinavia—has no supreme authority, the real cause of its peacefulness being that it is free from poverty and despotism. The same is true about internal peace: only countries where there is neither poverty nor despotism do not suffer from internal violence.

In conditions of misery, life, whether one's own or somebody else's, is not valued, and this facilitates greatly warlike propaganda. In an industrial society unemployment not only brings poverty but also breaks up social bonds and creates a large mass of uprooted men, whose frustrated desire for a place in society may lead them to favour measures of mass regimentation. Moreover, when there is not enough to satisfy the elementary needs of the population, the struggle for the good things of life becomes so bitter that democratic government, which always requires self-restraint and tolerance, becomes impossible, and despotism remains the only kind of government that can function at all. But absolute power creates the danger that a despot may push his country into war for the sake of satisfying his craving for power and glory. . . .

As far as ordinary people are concerned, who have to endure all the sufferings, their most important motives in supporting aggression are: (1) collective frenzy or (2) simple obedience combined with the herd spirit, or (3) a sense of desperate frustration which makes them covet other people's goods, and welcome all adventures. Usually these factors are intertwined. The mass movements assume forms of collective mania chiefly in response to extreme frustration of elementary needs, including the need to have a secure place in the social order. Such frustration is most commonly the consequence of poverty, or at least of impoverishment in relation to customary standards. If that is so we need not be surprised that war was a permanent and universal institution for poverty was, everywhere—and still is in most parts of the world—a permanent condition of the great majority. Only in very recent times, and only in the few fortunate countries bordering the north Atlantic has grinding poverty become rare.

It is evident that some struggle must always go on in human societies; but only if it is a struggle for the necessities of life must it involve killing. But why, we are bound to ask, do men always fight for the necessities of life? Why can they not just share them and live quietly? The answer to this has been given by Malthus.

The Malthusian Principle

The theory of Malthus has the privilege of being one of the very few sociological generalizations which possess the degree of certainty equal to that of the laws of physics. Indeed, its truth is no less certain than that of the statement that the earth is round. Its essence is simple in the extreme. Human population is biologically capable of doubling itself every generation, that is to say, about every twenty-five years. This, says Malthus, cannot go on for long because there is a limit to the amount of food any given territory, or the earth as a whole, can produce. Something must happen, therefore, either to the birth-rate or to the death-rate. Either some biologically possible births are prevented, or people must live a shorter time than they are biologically capable of living. . . .

In other words, high birth-rate must, in the long run, produce high death-rate, because population cannot grow indefinitely. A simple calculation shows that even if we started with a single couple the biological powers of procreation would be sufficient to cover the whole surface of the earth with human bodies in a few millennia. Even at the present rate of growth, which is certainly below the biologically possible maximum, the population

---

Population and Starvation

This natural tendency of the population to grow beyond the means of subsistence assured the permanence of bloody struggles. . . . The growth of population can produce war or some other form of strife long before the point of starvation is reached.

Stanislav Andreski

---

of the world would become so large before the lapse of two thousand years that there would be no room for people to stand on. . . .

This natural tendency of the population to grow beyond the means of subsistence assured the permanence of bloody struggles. Although sheer hunger has driven men into battle much more often than people brought up in opulent countries imagine, the growth of population can produce war or some other form of strife long before the point of starvation is reached: the mere drop from the customary standard of living may generate bellicose pulsions. Moreover, intensive warfare may keep the standard of living well above the subsistence level. . . . Many primitive tribes began to experience permanent starvation only after the pacification by the colonial governments.

The Origin of War

The recognition of this fact enables us to advance a hypothesis about the origin of war. As nothing of the sort exists among the mammals this institution must be the creation of culture. It probably came into existence when the advance in material culture enabled man to defend himself better against the beasts which preyed on him, and thus to disturb the natural balance which keeps the numbers of any species stationary in the long run. After the beasts had been subdued, another man became the chief obstacle in the search for food; and mutual killing began. A similar view has been expressed by a Chinese philosopher Han Fei-tzu (Circa fifth century B.C.) according to whom: "The men of old did not till the field, but the fruits of plants and trees were sufficient for food. Nor did the women weave, for the furs of birds and animals were enough for clothing. Without working there was enough to live, there were few people and plenty of supplies, and therefore the people did not quarrel. So neither large rewards nor heavy punishments were used, but the people governed themselves. But nowadays people do not consider a family of five children as large, and each child having again five children, before the death of the grandfather, there may be twenty-five grandchildren. The result is that there are many people and few supplies, that one has to work hard for a meagre return. So the people fall to quarrelling and though rewards may be doubled and punishments heaped up, one does not get away from disorder."

The remedies of signing treaties of eternal peace, convening congresses and preaching condemnation of wars, have been tried innumerable times and without much effect. They may be needed but in themselves are clearly insufficient. Elimination of poverty has not yet been tried except in very restricted areas where it had, in fact, the result of instilling into people a pacific disposition.

Given the propensities of human nature, the tendency of the population to grow beyond the resources has insured the ubiquity of wars, although not every single instance of war had this factor as an immediate cause. Wars might cease to be a permanent feature of social life only after the restoration of the demographic balance whose disappearance at an early stage of cultural development made them inevitable.

"I deeply believe that war is a sickness, though it may be mankind's sickness unto death."

War Is a Human Sickness

John G. Stoessinger

John G. Stoessinger received his Ph.D. from Harvard University (1954) and is currently professor of political science at the City University of New York. The author of numerous books on international relations, from 1967 to 1974 Dr. Stoessinger served as acting director of the Political Affairs Division at the United Nations. He also was chief book review editor of *Foreign Affairs* for five years and is a member of the Council on Foreign Relations. In the following viewpoint, Dr. Stoessinger draws upon six case studies to illustrate why he believes that "War Is a Human Sickness."

As you read, consider the following questions:

1. What six studies does the author rely upon to demonstrate his theory?
2. In what ways, according to the author do the personalities of leaders contribute to the outbreak of war?
3. After reading this viewpoint, explain why the author prefers to think of war as a human sickness.

Reprinted from WHY NATIONS GO TO WAR, 2nd Edition, by John G. Stoessinger. Copyright © 1978 by St. Martin's Press, Inc. Reprinted by permission of the publisher.

"If you look too deeply into the abyss," said Nietzsche, "the abyss will look into you." The face of war in our time is so awesome and so terrible that the first temptation is to recoil and turn away. Who of us has not despaired and concluded that the entire spectacle of war was a manifestation of organized insanity? . . .

Yet we must find the courage to confront the abyss. I deeply believe that war is a sickness, though it may be mankind's "sickness unto death." . . .

I know that the analogy between sickness and war is open to attack. It has been fashionable to assert that war is not an illness but, like aggression, an ineradicable part of human nature. I challenge this assumption. While aggression may be inherent in us all, war is learned behavior and, as such, can be unlearned and, ultimately, selected out entirely. . . .

We must therefore make an effort to look Medusa in the face and to diagnose the sickness. Diagnosis is no cure, of course, but it is the first and the most necessary step. I shall attempt this diagnosis by suggesting certain common themes from six case studies. . . .

Six Case Studies

The first general theme that compels attention is that no nation that began a major war in this century emerged a winner. Austria-Hungary and Germany, which precipitated World War I, went down to ignominious defeat; Hitler's Germany was crushed into unconditional surrender; the North Korean attack was thwarted by collective action and ended in a draw; although the Vietnam war ended in a Communist victory, it would be far too simple to blame the Communists exclusively for its beginning; the Arabs who invaded the new Jewish state in 1948 lost territory to the Israelis in four successive wars; and Pakistan, which wished to punish India through preemptive war, found itself dismembered in the process. In all cases, those who began a war came out a cropper. The nature or the ideology of the government that started a war seems to have made little, if any, difference. Defeat came to aggressors whether they were capitalists or Communists, white or non-white, Western or non-Western, rich or poor. . . .

In our time, unless the vanquished is destroyed completely, a victor's peace is seldom lasting. Those peace settlements that are negotiated on a basis of equality are much more permanent and durable. In 1918, Germany was defeated but not crushed. Versailles became the crucible for Hitler's Germany, which was then

70

brought down only through unconditional surrender. The Korean settlement was negotiated between undefeated equals. Both sides were unhappy, but neither side was so unhappy that it wished to overturn the settlement and initiate yet another war. An uneasy armistice or truce was gradually recognized as a possible basis for a peace settlement. The relative insecurity of each side thus became the guarantor of the relative security of both. Israel learned this lesson in October 1973. The victor's peace of 1967 had left the Arabs in a state of such frustration that they were compelled to try their hand once more at war. With their dignity restored in 1973, they found it psychologically possible to meet with Israelis in a face-to-face diplomatic encounter for the first time in a quarter of a century.

Personalities of Leaders

Turning to the problem of the outbreak of war, the case studies indicate the crucial importance of the personalities of

---

For Defense Only

If you study carefully the motives that lie behind the crucial decisions that led to World War I, you will find that, with the exception of France, all the other nations took physically aggressive action for defensive reasons. They felt that their very existence, or their national influence, power, or honor was threatened. All were frightened that if they did not go to war, they would cease to be world powers. A rage of impotence swept Europe, and we are currently locked into the same fearful stance.

Sue Mansfield, "War as the Ultimate Therapy," *Psychology Today*, June, 1982.

---

leaders. I am less impressed by the role of abstract forces such as nationalism, militarism, or alliance systems that traditionally have been regarded as the causes of war. Nor does a single one of the six cases indicate that economic factors played a vital part in precipitating war. The personalities of leaders, on the other hand, have often been decisive. . . .

The case material reveals that perhaps the most important single precipitating factor in the outbreak of war is misperception. Such distortion may manifest itself in four different ways: in a leader's image of himself; a leader's view of his adversary's character; a leader's view of his adversary's intentions toward himself; and, finally, a leader's view of his adversary's capabilities and power. Each of these is of such importance that it merits separate and careful treatment.

71

There is a remarkable consistency in the self-images of most national leaders on the brink of war. Each confidently expects victory after a brief and triumphant campaign. Doubt about the outcome is the voice of the enemy and therefore incomprehensible. This recurring atmosphere of optimism is not to be dismissed lightly by the historian as an ironic example of human folly. It assumes a powerful emotional momentum of its own and thus itself becomes one of the causes of war. Anything that fuels such optimism about a quick and decisive victory makes war more likely and anything that dampens it becomes a cause of peace.

This common belief in a short, decisive war is usually the overflow from a reservoir of self-delusions held by the leadership about both itself and nation. The Kaiser's appearance in shining armor in August 1914 and his promise to the German nation that its sons would be back home "before the leaves had fallen from the trees" was matched by similar scenes of overconfidence and military splendor in Austria, in Russia, and in the other nations on the brink of war. Hitler's confidence in an early German victory in Russia was so unshakable that no winter uniforms were issued to the soldiers and no preparations whatsoever made for the onset of the Russian winter. In November 1941, when the mud of autumn turned to ice and snow, the cold became the German soldier's bitterest enemy. Tormented by the Arctic temperatures, men died, machines broke down, and the quest for warmth all but eclipsed the quest for victory. Hitler's hopes and delusions about the German superman were shattered in the frozen wastes of Russia. The fact that Hitler had fought in World War I and seen that optimism crumble in defeat did not prevent its reappearance. When North Korea invaded South Korea, her leadership expected victory within two months. The Anglo-French campaign at Suez in 1956 was spurred by the hope of a swift victory. In Pakistan, Yahya Khan hoped to teach Indira Gandhi a lesson modelled on the Six-Day War in Israel. And in Vietnam, every American escalation in the air or on the ground was an expression of the hope that a few more bombs, a few more troops, would bring decisive victory.

Thus, leaders on all sides typically engage in self-delusions on the eve of war. Only the war itself then provides the stinging ice of reality and ultimately helps restore a measure of perspective in the leadership. The price for this recapture of reality is high indeed. It is unlikely that there ever was a war that fulfilled the initial hopes and expectations of both sides. . . .

Paranoid Leadership

If a leader on the brink of war believes that his adversary will attack him, the chances of war are fairly high. If both leaders share this perception about each other's intent, war becomes a virtual certainty. The mechanism of the self-fulfilling prophecy is then set in motion. If leaders attribute evil designs to their adversaries, and if they nurture these beliefs for long enough, they will eventually be proven right. . . .

A leader's misperception of his adversary's power is perhaps the quintessential cause of war. It is vital to remember, however, that it is not the actual distribution of power that precipitates a war; it is the way in which a leader thinks that power is distributed. A war will start when nations disagree over their perceived strength. The war itself then becomes a dispute over measurement. Reality is gradually restored as war itself cures war. And the war will end when the fighting nations perceive each other's strength more realistically. . . .

Thus, on the eve of each war, at least one nation misperceives another's power. In that sense, the beginning of each war is a misperception or an accident. The war itself then slowly, and in agony, teaches men about reality. And peace is made when reality has won. The outbreak of war and the coming of peace are separated by a road that leads from misperception to reality. The

'Ya hear that, boys — the kid asks if it's a profession with a future'

C.P. Houston, *Houston Chronicle*. Reprinted with permission.

most tragic aspect of this truth is that war has continued to remain the best teacher of reality and thus has been the most effective cure for war.

Recognizing Statements That Are Provable

From various sources of information we are constantly confronted with statements and generalizations about social and moral problems. In order to think clearly about these problems, it is useful if one can make a basic distinction between statements for which evidence can be found and other statements which cannot be verified or proved because evidence is not available, or the issue is so controversial that it cannot be definitely proved.

Readers should constantly be aware that magazines, newspapers and other sources often contain statements of a controversial nature. The following activity is designed to allow experimentation with statements that are provable and those that are not.

Most of the following statements are taken from the viewpoints in this chapter. Consider each statement carefully. *Mark P for any statement you believe is provable. Mark U for any statement you feel is unprovable because of the lack of evidence. Mark C for statements you think are too controversial to be proved to everyone's satisfaction.*

If you are doing this activity as a member of a class or group, compare your answers with those of other class or group members. Be able to defend your answers. You may discover that others will come to different conclusions than you. Listening to the reasons others present for their answers may give you valuable insights in recognizing statements that are provable.

If you are reading this book alone, ask others if they agree with your answers. You too will find this interaction very valuable.

> $P = provable$
> $U = unprovable$
> $C = too \ controversial$

1. The complexity and vastness of modern bureaucratic government complicates the issue of personal responsibility.

2. The slow tentative progress human beings have made in the direction of civilization has been overwhelmed by the phenomenal advances in lethal technology.

3. It is a metaphor to say that technology dictates policy, for people, not machines, make the decisions.

4. Genetically we have not evolved very strikingly since Cro-Magnon man, but culturally we have changed beyond recognition.

5. Our soldiers are bullied into all-out fighting by penalizing fleeing in battle.

6. Man's limited behavioral adjustability has been outpaced by the culturally determined changes in his social environment and that is why man is now a misfit in his own society.

7. We crave scapegoats, targets to absorb our self doubts, our feelings of hopelessness.

8. We'll always have wars, where you have a lot of people not having their next meal to take for granted.

9. War originated long before the art of writing.

10. The remedy against war is to institute a world government.

11. War has been blamed on human nature, and it is perfectly true that if all men were kind and wise there would be no wars.

12. It is evident that some struggle must always go on in human societies.

13. It must be remembered that wars against rebels constituted, next to external wars, the chief occupation of governments throughout history.

14. No nation that began a major war in this century emerged a winner.

15. While aggression may be inherent in us all, war is learned behavior and, as such, can be unlearned.

Bibliography

The following list of books deals with the subject matter of this chapter.

Arendt, Hannah — *On Violence*, New York: Harcourt, Brace and World, 1970.

Bernad, Luther L. — *War and Its Causes*, New York: Garland Publishing, Inc., 1944.

Blackett, Patrick M. — *Studies of War: Nuclear and Conventional*, Westport, CT: Greenwood, 1978.

Blainey, Geoffrey — *The Causes of War*, New York: Free Press, 1975.

Brodie, Bernard — *War and Politics*, New York: MacMillan, 1973.

Dickinson, Goldsworthy L. — *Causes of International War*, New York: Garland Publishing, Inc., 1972.

Melman, Seymour — *The Permanent War Economy*, Austin, TX: S&S Press, 1976.

Morel, Edmund D. — *Truth and the War*, New York: Garland Publishing, Inc., 1972.

Nelson, Keith L. — *Why War?* Berkeley, CA: University of California Press, 1979.

Rose, John P. — *The Evolution of US Army Nuclear Doctrine 1945-1980*, Boulder, CO: Westview, 1980.

Schell, Jonathan — *The Fate of the Earth*, New York: Alfred A. Knopf, 1982.

Shinn, Roger L. — *Wars and Rumors of Wars*, New York: Abingdon Press, 1972.

Taylor, A. J. — *How Wars Begin*, New York: Atheneum, 1979.

Thomas, Norman — *No Glory, No Profit, No Need*, New York: Garland Publishing, Inc., 1972.

Is Nuclear War Justifiable?

"Those who pray that they will never have to use nuclear weapons must be willing to use them if necessary."

Nuclear War Is Justifiable

Kenneth S. Kantzer

Kenneth Kantzer, a long-time educator and philosopher, is president of Trinity College, Deerfield, Illinois and is a former editor of *Christianity Today*. He received his Ph.D. in philosophy and religion from Harvard University and has written and edited numerous essays including the book *Evangelical Roots*. In the following viewpoint, Mr. Kantzer, while acknowledging the catastrophic effects of nuclear war, argues that there are values which must transcend human physical life.

As you read, consider the following questions:

1. According to the author, why is the just war concept complicated by nuclear weapons?
2. Does the author appear to place "physical human life" as his highest value?
3. What does the author believe are the alternatives to the buildup and use of nuclear weapons?
4. According to the author, what "moral and rational choice" are we left with?

Americans generally, and evangelicals particularly, are confused and troubled by the debate over nuclear armament and the threat of nuclear war. And well they might be! In World War I, 15 million people died. In World War II, 51 million people died. With proportional increases for World War III, 150 million will die, and many Americans will be in that number. Such a dreadful prospect surely demands clear, hard-headed thinking with a heart-felt appeal to a merciful God for wisdom and guidance.

Long ago, the vast majority of evangelicals became convinced that war is not always wrong. Drawing on the clear teaching of both Testaments, they concluded that there is such a thing as a moral right—even duty—to serve as a soldier. The biblical evidence is set forth in such passages as Romans 13. There the apostle Paul teaches that civil authority functions as "the servant of God to execute his wrath on the wrongdoer." Thus, when a government uses force to defend the rights of its citizens, it is doing "good" and is approved by God himself. Throughout both Old and New Testaments, the taking of life under certain circumstances is approved. . . .

Jesus' teaching about loving our enemies and his warning against personal vengeance were intended to guide personal relations but not to deny governments the right to use force. . . .

Some wars are right. In World War II, 51 million people died in a tragedy so terrible that our minds can scarcely take it in, but it was right to battle against Hitler and a world dominated by the Nazis. . . .

Accordingly, the church has seen fit not to rule out all war as wrong but to stress its moral parameters and to struggle desperately for peace.

Complicating Factor: Nuclear War

Today many evangelicals are asking whether modern nuclear warfare does not make just wars impossible. The fact is, they say, nuclear war cannot be limited; so, ipso facto, there can be no just war.

Nuclear warfare, for example, is essentially indiscriminate, but to some extent so is all warfare. The siege of a nation's city brought starvation to all within its walls, and invariably the women and children died first. And the military has often sought to safeguard its forces by identification with civilian population. But the principle is right. We must never aim to kill innocent people; we must protect them from harm as much as possible. This parameter of conventional warfare ought to be insisted on in all nuclear engagement. Therefore, we should pledge that we will not aim our nuclear warheads at civilian populations—no matter what the provocation. Naturally, this will no more guarantee that civilians will remain unharmed than it has in the past. But it will limit civilian losses to attacks directed against military establishments. We should renounce any retaliations in kind, even for an opponent's bombing of our civilian population. It is always wrong to intend to kill the innocent.

Again, it is often argued that in the event of nuclear war we have no guarantee against ultimate escalation. Each side will seek to guarantee its victories by larger and larger threats and greater and greater reprisals until the ultimate destruction of an entire population is certain to be the end result. Naturally, we cannot determine what our opponents will do, but we can at least determine what we will *not* do. . . .

Finally, will the end justify going to war in a nuclear exchange when so many millions will almost certainly be destroyed? Here everything hangs on our relative values. We do not have many Patrick Henrys who prefer liberty to death. If physical human life is our highest value, then certainly we must abjure not only nuclear war, but also conventional war.

Bomb if We Must

In the contest between bullydom and human rights, one aspect which tends to tip the balance in favor of bullies is the fact that they can rely on the extreme reluctance of good people ever to *use* weapons causing mass-slaughter, no matter what outrages the bullies commit. The very decency of good people can leave human rights without a credible defense. Today, if good people refuse to use nuclear weapons, they are unilaterally disarmed no matter how many such weapons they possess.

John W. Gofman and Egan O'Connor, *On the Morality of Weapons,* April 1982.

But the evangelical is not committed to human physical life as the highest value. As he contemplates what it will mean to live in the Gulag societies described by Solzhenitsyn, 100 million deaths may not be too great a price to pay. That depends on how much we value the freedom to rear our children in religious faith and to preserve for some a measure of political and social freedom. . . .

Alternative: Universal Conscription

Fact is, the free world has inadequate nonnuclear deterrents to Soviet expansionism. To renounce all use of nuclear weapons,

81

therefore, is to leave just two options: (1) "The Great Surrender," involving absolute capitulation; or (2) immediate universal conscription and the buildup of conventional arms and enormous expense that would transform the United States into a military state more like the Soviet Union. This could be done. The Swiss people have done it for many decades They allocate over a third of their national budget for military expenses and support universal conscription with regular military stints each year required of all males to the age of 47.

Do we want this? The rejection of all nuclear weapons must be faced forthrightly. If its proponents are really advocating capitulation and the loss of our basic freedoms, they should say so. If they would "rather be Red than dead," it is their privilege in a free society to say so. Or, if they really would prefer to have universal conscription in America, with an immense buildup of conventional arms, radical transformation of our whole economy, and the treat of a nearly Russian-like poverty, that too is their privilege. But the alternatives should be faced openly and debated without subterfuge. At the present time, tactical nuclear weapons are the only deterrent against the vast and impressive Russian military establishment.

Sometimes the objection to tactical nuclear warheads seems to rest on a careless disregard of the awfulness of conventional warfare. But past history warns us that even a conventional war might destroy a quarter of a billion people. Western Europe in particular is much better protected by the nuclear umbrella that prevents its destruction by conventional weapons. . . .

Some object that a limited nuclear deterrent will simply not deter. But it has! As Churchill wisely noted, atomic weapons have brought us a measure of peace. That peace has now stretched out for over 30 years. Under God, such a deterrent has alone kept the peace. Pray God that it may buy us time while we work sincerely and desperately for a more firm basis for peace.

Moreover, a similar situation worked in the Second World War. Each side possessed a huge stockpile of poison gas. Neither side employed it because each knew that the other side would certainly reply in kind. Even in his final days Hitler was not able effectively to turn to gas warfare as a last desperate recourse. . . .

Limited Nuclear Defense

It would seem to me, therefore, that we really have only one moral and rational choice. That is to rely upon a strictly limited nuclear defense while at the same time working desperately toward the goal of a nuclear freeze — and then a nuclear cutback, and then an outlawing of nuclear weapons; the ultimate goal would be the destruction of conventional weapons. But those who pray that they will never have to use nuclear weapons must be willing to use them if necessary. Otherwise, there is no deterrent, but only a unilateral disarmament leading through appeasement and surrender to slavery.

We must beware of those who cry, "Peace, peace!" but who would only lead us down a primrose path to slavery or poverty and, in the end, war. Freedom and peace are precious pearls of great price. But they come only to those who are willing to fight for them — and who pray that by God's grace they will not have to.

"Can anyone seriously conceive of Jesus dropping nuclear bombs or launching an ICBM which would kill or cripple thousands of mothers and children?"

Nuclear War Is Not Justifiable

Reo M. Christenson

Reo Christenson has written extensively on political subjects and has authored several books, the most recent being *American Politics*. He is professor of political science at Miami University in Oxford, Ohio. In the following viewpoint, Mr. Christenson takes the position of the modern Christian pacifist and argues that nuclear war can never be justified. Tyranny, he contends, can be resisted through nonviolent means.

As you read, consider the following questions:

1. According to the author, what position did many early Christian writers hold on war?
2. What was St. Augustine's theory on war and what is its historical significance?
3. What is the author's opinion of Kenneth Kantzer's editorial in *Christianity Today*?
4. Do you agree with the author? Why or why not?

The issue of the nuclear freeze has created a lively interest in the broader question of the Christian's general attitude toward war. Unless I misread the signals, there is a growing tendency to question the long-dominant Christian stand on this issue. In an age in which warfare can be destructive beyond anything previously imagined, should Christians support even a "just-war" philosophy? Should they have done so before the nuclear age? . . .

The earliest Christians did not serve in the armed forces. Roland Bainton notes that "from the end of the New Testament period to the decade A.D. 170-180 there is no evidence whatever of Christians in the army" (*Christian Attitudes Toward War and Peace*). In recent, eminently scholarly review of the evidence, Louis J. Swift notes that while prayers for the empire were common in the second century, ". . .there was a general condemnation of warfare or at least of Christian participation in combat." Swift says Justin Martyr "takes it as a matter of course that Christians refrain from violent acts." He declares that Origen viewed wars as "incompatible with the doctrines of Christ," that Tertullian opposed war as a matter of pacifist principle, and that "Lactantius was a pacifist in the usual and strict sense of the word." Swift concludes that, contrary to the inadequately researched views of some writers, "the real issue for those Christian writers who dealt with the problem of war at any length was not idolatry or eschatology or antagonism to the empire but simply the notion that killing and love were incompatible." Since the erosions of time and tradition had only minimally affected their faith, the early Christian writers' perception of Jesus' message is not to be lightly dismissed as we seek to ascertain the appropriate Christian posture toward war.

The Importance of Augustine

Only gradually did Christians abandon their opposition to military service, as Rome became Christianized and the barbarians swung down from the north. St. Augustine's doctrine that "just war" was consistent with Christian principles, a theory that built on assumptions that had been gradually developing within the church, was finally accepted by most of the Christian world. St. Augustine found warfare an acceptable activity for Christians if the war had been initiated by the proper authorities, was designed to restore peace and promote justice, if it avoided wanton violence and looting—and if it was fought by Christians in a spirit of "benevolent severity" rather than of hatred. . . .

St. Augustine's theory may have been the most momentous

development in the history of post-Pauline Christendom. Its consequences are difficult to exaggerate, and its impact upon Christian attitudes and behavior is immeasurable. Once Augustine endorsed "just war" as authorizing Christians' participation in military activities, "just war" soon became whatever war their government engaged in. . . .

I understand why Christians have defended war. The Old Testament provides numerous examples of wars seemingly sanctioned or ordered by Yahweh. Nor is the New Testament

LEANING TOWER!

Ollie Harrington, *Daily World.*

evidence against war as crystal-clear as many of us would wish. John the Baptist did not tell the soldier to put down his arms but "to do violence to no man, neither accuse any falsely; and be content with your wages." Acts 10:7 refers to a "devout soldier," and Cornelius had soldiers under his authority.

John the Baptist's admonition to the soldiers "to do violence to no man" is not inconsistent with Christian pacifism, of course. And it should be remembered that soldiers in New Testament times typically played the role of policemen, a function every society needs.

The Scriptures and Violence

In reviewing the New Testament record in terms of its most fundamental ethical message, however, one can make a strong case that most Christians have misperceived the major thrust of scriptural teachings on the use of violence. Consider the following:

1. Whatever is recorded in the Old Testament, there are no chosen people anymore. Nor does God provide material instructions or exhortations to any favored nation.

2. Where passages of Scripture may seem to be at odds with one another, the most reliable way to resolve the apparent differences is through testing them against the teachings and example of Jesus. He is the most trustworthy interpreter and exemplar of the mind and will of God. We follow the safest and surest course when we turn to his life and his counsel for guidance.

3. The most distinctive aspect of Jesus' moral teachings is his emphasis not only on loving one's neighbor as oneself but on doing good to one's enemies, praying for them and forgiving them for their trespasses against one. Many non-Christian religions concur in the other ethical teachings of Jesus, but the emphasis placed on this principle is not only basic to Christianity but the most beautiful ethical dimension of the Christian message. It directly challenges our unregenerate instincts while appealing to the finest that is in us. One feels a powerful sense that this principle does more to confirm the validity of the Christian message than anything but the incarnation and the resurrection.

The human mind is remarkably resourceful in rationalizing what it wishes to believe. Yet it takes an almost preposterous amount of sophistry to argue that we can love our enemies and do good to them while maiming and butchering them, together with their families. If this is loving our enemies, then how does love differ from hatred? . . .

4. I realize that it is often pointless to speculate about what Jesus would do if he were here today. Those speculations often reflect only a particular family background and religious orientation. Still, I do not believe it is amiss to apply what we know about Jesus' teachings and example to war—especially to modern war.

Can anyone seriously conceive of Jesus hurling hand grenades at his enemies, using a machine gun, manipulating a flamethrower, dropping nuclear bombs or launching an ICBM which would kill or cripple thousands of mothers and children? The question is so absurd that it scarcely merits an answer. If Jesus could not do this and be true to his character, then how can we do it and be true to him? . . .

Kenneth Kantzer, former editor and now advisory editor of *Christianity Today*, recently wrote an editorial in that journal (January 21) in which he defended Christian support for nuclear war, if that war seemed necessary to national defense: "100 million deaths may not be too great a price to pay," he said. Why? Because he implicitly accepts Augustine's "just-war" theory and because "I value my freedoms of speech and press

---

A Moral Imperative

I am told by some that unilateral disarmament in the face of atheistic communism is insane. I find myself observing that nuclear armament by anyone is itself atheistic, and anything but sane. I am also told that the choice of unilateral disarmament is a political impossibility in this country. If so, perhaps the reason is that we have forgotten what it would be like to act out of faith. But I speak here of that choice not as a political platform—it might not win elections—but as a moral imperative.

Raymond G. Hunthausen, *Faith and Disarmament*, a speech delivered to the Pacific Northwest Synod for the Lutheran Church, June 12, 1981.

---

and religion more than life. To teach my children about God is more important to me than life itself. I would rather not bring children into the world than to give them birth only to have them reared as Marxist atheists.". . .

If Kantzer is willing to accept 100 million deaths as the price willingly paid to continue living under our political system, presumably 200 million would also be acceptable. Or any number whatever, since he not only values liberty "more than life itself" but is willing to kill and injure as many people as is necessary to protect that liberty.

If the privilege of raising one's children in freedom is worth 100 million or more lives in a nuclear war, this raises another question. Is it less important for Russian parents to be able freely to teach their children about God than it is for American parents to do so? Not if we love others as we do ourselves. Then would not an American war against Russia be justified in order to destroy a godless system and install one with religious and political freedom — even if 100 million or more lives were lost thereby? Such a "holy war" would seem to be logically justified by Kantzer's premises and reasoning.

Nonviolent Alternatives

Certainly Christians would be faithless to their mission if they cooperated with a communist aggressor who sought to deprive them of their rights to freedom of worship, freedom of speech and freedom of choice in all that matters, while that aggressor imposed a ruthless totalitarian system on the people.

To carry this position a step further: Should Christians stand idly by when tyranny strikes from within rather than from without? Who believes that Christians should have supinely accepted the Nazi campaign to round up and exterminate the Jews? Should they not have risked their lives instead, not by slaying the Nazis, but by shielding the Jews at whatever cost to themselves? And should they not have spoken out in condemnation of the Nazis when the latter sought to subjugate the churches by imposing their will on them? We honor the Christians who took this stand, who courageously practiced nonviolent resistance when Hitler committed his barbarous crimes against the German people.

An aggressor nation could, of course, readily overrun a people who declined to meet force with force. But it could not enslave them against their will. You are a slave only if you permit yourself to be a slave. If one resists illegitimate power, one may be beaten, imprisoned or killed. But one will not be enslaved. And soldiers, one might add, find little gratification or glory in gunning down those who, with dignity and courage, resist evil through nonviolent means. If anything is likely to make aggressors reflect upon the propriety of their deeds, it is that spectacle. No behavior would be more likely to unsettle, confuse and even to conquer the conquerors than this kind of courage and commitment to principle.

"Our nation's only hope of remaining free is to be prepared to go to war even at the risk of being destroyed."

Nuclear War May Be Necessary

H.O.J. Brown & George Mavrodes

The "Better red than dead" comment inspires considerable debate among public figures and authors; among them Harold O. J. Brown and George Mavrodes. Dr. Brown is the author of several books on ethics and society, such as *Christianity and the Class Struggle*, and is a professor of systematic theology at Trinity Divinity School. Mr. Mavrodes is widely known for his original analyses of difficult ethical problems and is a philosophy professor at the University of Michigan. In the following viewpoint, the authors argue that there *are* reasons for which a nation should be prepared to go to nuclear war.

As you read, consider the following questions:

1. Why does Mr. Brown believe that Christians "are the free world's hope of remaining free?"
2. What does Mr. Mavrodes mean by "morality of chances?"
3. Do you agree with the authors? Why or why not?

"Rumors of War", June 1980. Reprinted by permission of ETERNITY Magazine, Copyright 1980, Evangelical Ministries, Inc., 1716 Spruce Street, Philadelphia, PA 19103.

I

Along with most of those who accept the just war theory that a war of national self-defense is compatible with God's laws, I do not believe Christians should be categorical pacifists even in our generation, even with the possibility of mass destruction by nuclear weapons.

A war between the United States and the Soviet Union, with or without the involvement of Communist China, would be terribly destructive and might actually eradicate human civilization or human life itself. Yet failure to resist the Soviet Union might subjugate the entire world to the most odious of tyrannies. In a fallen world, and confronting a determined adversary such as the Soviet Union, our nation's only hope of remaining free is to be prepared to go to war to defend itself, even at the risk of being destroyed. The monstrous evil of totalitarian Communism must indeed be frightful—as it is—for us to risk annihilation rather than submit to it. Frankly, I agree with Aleksandr Solzhenitsyn and will risk annihilation for myself and for my country to defend our freedom.

Fortunately, Soviet Union rulers seem intent not on causing a nuclear war but on getting all they can short of it. For this reason one can at least hope that a high level of military preparedness, coupled with a willingness to fight even a nuclear war, offers at least some prospects of preserving freedom and avoiding universal destruction.

I believe we should make it quite clear to the U.S.S.R. where we draw the line. It is reasonable to draw it when vital United States interests—such as the energy supply of the free world—are being jeopardized. If one is going to draw the line, one must be in a position to fight effectively, which is hardly the case with the United States at the present time. The past three administrations have brought about severe weakening of our military capabilities. Whether this trend can be reversed in time to deter the Soviet Union from launching ever-more-threatening aggressions is not apparent, but it seems to me we have no choice but to try.

Christians, unlike secularists, have the great consolation that they can try conscientiously to do their best without being in a panic about the outcome—which is after all in the hands of God, who will save all who trust in Christ, war or no war. In one way, perhaps it is the Christians who are the free world's hope of remaining free, for it is we alone who can dare to risk losing much or all in war to forestall what we consider a still greater evil, the world domination of a totalitarian, atheistic system as pictured by George Orwell in *Nineteen Eighty-Four*.

In my opinion a proper *causus belli* for a just war has already existed a number of times. So far we have been able to refrain from military action, for example in Iran, without suffering grievously in consequence. There will come a time, however, when our perceived weakness will embolden enemies of various kinds to menace us in ways we cannot ignore. For this reason it is important to have at least some Christians in positions of authority, people who will not be "kept in bondage by the fear of death," as Hebrews puts it. The slogan, "Better dead than red," will not guarantee our death, but, "Better red than dead," will almost surely bring our enslavement.

II

Many Christians—"just-war theorists"—who have considered when a nation might properly engage in warfare have said that, among other things, there should be some good purpose accomplished by the warfare, and the means used should not be out of proportion to that purpose.

Formally, the means were taken simply to be the fighting of the war itself. The main problems were estimating in advance the benefits and costs to both oneself and the enemy and then putting these in perspective for comparison. Modern warfare, however, because it is enormously destructive and potentially worldwide in scope, has made prominent another problem—one to which Christians have given comparatively little thought. That is the notion of *deterrence*. How can we best prevent attack and retaliation? This concept generates special problems.

For example, say the U.S. tries to deter the Soviet Union from launching a nuclear attack. We do so by threatening that, if attacked, we will strike back with nuclear weapons. Is that threat works—if the Societs really are deterred—it looks like a great bargain. We have achieved a very good result just by making a threat.

But what if it does not work? What if the Soviets *do* launch their attack? Then there is tremendous suffering and death in the U.S. And after that? Could we then *properly* strike back, as we threatened? A conventional application of just-war theory makes it doubtful, for the counter-strike will simply add Russian suffering to American suffering. It would not prevent American suffering.

More generally, deterrence is accomplished—if at all—by the

92

threat of retaliation. But if things get to the point where the retaliatory act is actually *done*, then the deterrence fails. How then is the retaliatory act to be justified?

It is this relation between the threat, the credibility of the threat, and the actual doing of the retaliatory act which generates the special moral problems surrounding deterrence.

At this point, bluffing may look morally attractive. Threaten to retaliate, but—if push comes to shove—do not actually do it. Against a determined and knowledgeable adversary, such as the Soviet Union, however, bluffing is unlikely to work for long especially in a relatively "open" society like ours.

"Morality of Chances"

My own view is that traditional formulations of just-war theory need to be supplemented here by the idea of a "morality of chances." When we think about deterrence then, the means whose cost we should consider is not our *actual* counter-strike. It is rather the *chance* of such a counter-strike. What we impose on the Soviet Union, in an attempt to achieve some good end, is a certain chance, a certain probability, of nuclear destruction. And then the general pattern of just-war thinking can be applied to this new idea of the means.

Greater of Two Evils

Any of the wide variety of possible uses of nuclear weapons would be dreadful. However, it is reckless to decree that any use, even any possession for deterrence purposes, is necessarily a larger evil than the long night of centuries that would follow the extinguishing of Western cultural values by armed totalitarianism.

George F. Will, "Nuclear Morality," *Newsweek*, December 21, 1981.

Generally, if something has a certain cost, then a *chance* of that thing will have a lower cost. If a prize is worth a dollar, then a lottery ticket for that prize will generally be worth less than a dollar. If my house is sure to burn down this year, then it is worth a lot to insure it. But if it has only a small chance of burning down, then an insurance policy is worth much less.

In a similar way, nuclear strike against the Soviet Union would impose, and therefore "cost," an enormous Russian suffering. A ten percent chance of such a strike, however, should be assigned ten percent of that cost. And that might make an important difference. For suppose we estimate that by threatening a counter-strike—and really being ready and determined to do it—we have a ninety percent chance of deterring a similar attack on the U.S. The good purpose to be achieved, then, is equal to avoiding ninety percent of the U.S. destruction. The cost of the means is equal to ten percent of the Soviet destruction. And that means may very well turn out to be "proportionate" and just according to just-war theory.

This requires, of course, an additional estimate: that of the probability of succeeding and failing. Some people will find this distasteful, and it is certainly difficult to do. But that is not exclusive to war. Life is full of chances, and we are continuously required to balance one chance against another. Christians, too, must face that task, in warfare as elsewhere.

If we decide to take this chance, *then we must really take it.* No bluffing—it will not work. In this case, it means putting our rockets on the line, with the solemn realization that there is a real chance they will go off.

In my opinion it is worth doing that to deter a Soviet attack on the U.S. It is probably also worth doing it against major Soviet expansion into areas crucial to the U.S. But it is not worth doing against every Soviet incursion against its neighbors. It is part of the historical tragedy of some nations and some people that they live within the Soviet shadow. We cannot now prevent every such tragedy. And there are some ways in which we cannot try. But for some things we can, and should, accept this risk.

"No all-out nuclear war can ever be a just war and no provocation . . . can justify our beginning one."

Nuclear War Could Never Be Necessary

Lewis B. Smedes & Arthur F. Holmes

When asked "Under what circumstances would you feel you could morally support a war with the Soviet Union?" two Christian ethicists responded that no circumstances would warrant it. These two men discuss the hypothetical situation of escalation into a nuclear war and the likely consequences. Both are professors. Lewis B. Smedes teaches Christian ethics at Fuller Seminary and Arthur F. Holmes, editor of a book of readings on topics of a just war entitled *War and Christian Ethics*, teaches philosophy at Wheaton College.

As you read, consider the following questions:

1. According to Mr. Smedes, under what conditions can war be justified?
2. According to Mr. Holmes, what conditions make the use of force morally wrong?
3. Do you agree with the authors? Why or why not?

"Rumors of War", June 1980. Reprinted by permission of ETERNITY Magazine, Copyright 1980, Evangelical Ministries, Inc., 1716 Spruce Street, Philadelphia, PA 19103.

I

We cannot speculate about the conditions under which it might be possible to begin a war without asking what that war would do to us before it was finished. We cannot simply ask about conditions that would justify starting a war; we must ask about the kind of war we are likely to end up fighting. The question then must be: "What conditions would justify an all-out nuclear war between the great powers?" for that is what any war with the Soviet Union would likely become.

Surely we would soon escalate any war with the Soviets into a nuclear war. On that assumption, I am hard-pressed to imagine any provocation so serious as to justify it. War can be justified only if it is fought with a goal of righting wrongs or restoring just relationships between nations, and with a force measured to that end. But what chance is there of restoring a just relationship between two nations when the force used destroys both of them as viable states? If we fight to preserve our freedoms, what have we accomplished if we kill almost all the people who might have enjoyed those freedoms? If we fight to protect our vital interests, what have we accomplished if we kill most of the interested people? If we fight for our nation's survival, what have we accomplished if we destroy ourselves in the effort? No, I cannot find in my imagination's storehouse anything to justify all-out nuclear war.

If it is still possible to fight a conventional war, comparable, let us say, to World War II, we would face another sort of tradeoff. An all-out war, short of nuclear exchange, would still inflict such grotesque suffering on both peoples, along with their neighbors, that it is still all but impossible to foresee a justifiable provocation so terrible. The devastation, spread over most of the world, lasting years, could not balance most offenses the Soviet Union might be guilty of doing. If the Russian soldiers landed on our coast, with intent to conquer us, I would be in favor of fighting. Short of this, perhaps only a direct and massive assault on Western Europe would justify, in my conscience, a total war.

I am, of course, talking principle. I do not pretend to know the best way to convince Russia to decline any temptation to expand into areas that the United States considers vital to its survival as an energy-hungry society. Who knows, maybe the best way to avoid a war is to persuade the Russians we are willing to fight one. This is the kind of question that requires a statesman more than a moralist. In our sinfully disordered world, such devious

WORLD WAR III MEMORIAL

Robert Englehart, *Hartford Courant.* Reprinted with permission.

tactics may be necessary for peace.

Since it is hard to imagine a war with Russia that would not mushroom into a total conflict, our Christian task is to proclaim the modern truth about just wars. This truth is that *no* all-out nuclear war can ever be a just war, and that no provocation by any nation can justify our beginning one.

II

From the standpoint of a just war theory, the only legitimate cause for going to war is for defense against violent aggression. The only just intention can be the restoration of a just peace, not ideological, religious, or economic ends. And the just conduct of war both forbids means disproportionate to the evil they seek to avert, and insists on immunity of noncombatants from intentional attack. If reasonable hope of success within these limits is not possible, then the use of military force is morally wrong.

Consequently, while I can see resisting Soviet aggression in a limited or localized sphere, "total warfare" is unthinkable. In particular, strategic nuclear weapons (counter-city) have been denounced by Christian ethicists, Protestant and Catholic, as a crime against God and man; and tactical nuclear weapons could too easily trigger further escalation. I cannot see how a world war with modern weaponry could ever again be justified.

As for defending an Iran or a Pakistan, this would be entirely unwarranted apart from a mutual defense treaty or an explicit and official plea for help; but I doubt our military is wanted there any more than the Soviets' presence. and our own economic interests are insufficient reason for war.

a basic reading and thinking skill

Understanding Words in Context

Readers occasionally come across words which they do not recognize. And frequently, because the reader does not know a word or words, he or she will not fully understand the passage being read. Obviously, the reader can look up an unfamiliar word in a dictionary. However, by carefully examining the word in the context in which it is used, the word's meaning can often be determined. A careful reader may find clues to the meaning of the word in surrounding words, ideas and attitudes.

Below are ten excerpts from the viewpoints in this chapter. In each excerpt, one or two words are printed in italics. Try to determine the meaning of each word by reading the excerpt. Under each excerpt you will find four definitions for the italicized word. Choose the one that is closest to your understanding of the word.

Finally, use a dictionary to see how well you have understood the words in context. It will be helpful to discuss with others the clues which helped you decide each word's meaning.

1. The [Swiss] *ALLOCATE* over a third of their national budget for military expenses.

    ALLOCATE means:
    a) to find
    b) continue
    c) to set apart
    d) decide upon

2. We must never aim to kill innocent people; we must protect them from harm as much as possible. This *PARAMETER* of conventional warfare ought to be insisted on in all nuclear engagements.

    PARAMETER means:
    a) a determining factor
    b) accessability
    c) small favor
    d) permission

3. It takes an almost preposterous amount of *SOPHISTRY* to argue that we can love our enemies and do good to them while maiming and butchering them, together with their families.

SOPHISTRY means:
a) physical force
b) kindness
c) clever persuasion
d) people

4. Should they not have spoken out in condemnation of the Nazis when the latter sought to *SUBJUGATE* the churches by imposing their will on them?

SUBJUGATE means:
a) condemn
b) bring under control
c) refuse to cooperate
d) greatly assist

5. I do not believe Christians should be *CATEGORICAL* pacifists even in our generation, even with the possibility of mass destruction by nuclear weapons.

CATEGORICAL means:
a) ignorant
b) unconditional
c) educated
d) learned

6. A high level of military preparedness, coupled with a willingness to fight even a nuclear war, offers at least some prospects preserving freedom and avoiding *UNIVERSAL* destruction.

UNIVERSAL means:
a) in part
b) small
c) outer space
d) occurring everywhere

7. Surely we would soon escalate any war with the Soviets into a nuclear war. On that assumption, I am hard-pressed to imagine any *PROVOCATION* so serious as to justify it.

PROVOCATION means:
a) leave alone
b) pull apart
c) call forth action
d) mistake

8. An all-out war, short of nuclear exchange, would still inflict such *GROTESQUE* suffering on both peoples, along with their neighbors.

GROTESQUE means:
a) not likely
b) fantastic, bizarre
c) somewhat pleasant
d) mean, sinister

Bibliography

The following list of books deals with the subject matter of this chapter.

Adams, Ruth and Cullen, Susan, eds.	*The Final Epidemic: Physicians and Scientists on Nuclear War*, Chicago: The Educational Foundation for Nuclear Science, 1981.
Beckman, Petr	*The Health Hazards of Not Going Nuclear*, New York: Ace Books, 1980.
Cohen, S. T.	*The Neutron Bomb*, Cambridge, MA: Institute for Foreign Policy Analysis, 1978.
Dando, M. and Newman, B., eds.	*Nuclear Deterrence: Implications & Policy Options for the 1980s*, Atlantic Highlands, NJ: Humanities, 1982.
Etzold, Thomas H.	*Defense or Delusion?* New York: Harper & Row, 1982.
Goodwin, Geoffrey	*Ethics and Nuclear Deterrence*, New York: St. Martin, 1982.
Goodwin, Peter	*Nuclear War: The Facts of Our Survival*, New York: The Rutledge Press, 1981.
Holmes, Arthur R., ed.	*War and Christian Ethics*, Grand Rapids, MI: Baker Books House Company, 1975.
Kaplan, Fred	*The Wizards of Armageddon*, New York: Simon & Schuster, 1983.
Katz, Arthur M.	*Life After Nuclear War*, Cambridge, MA: Ballinger Publishing, 1982.
Luzin, N.	*Nuclear Strategy & Common Sense*, (Progress Publishers, USSR) Chicago: Imported Publications, 1981.
McNaught, L. W.	*Nuclear, Biological & Chemical Warfare*, Elmsford, NY: Pergamon, 1982.
Unipublishers	*Comprehensive Study on Nuclear Weapons*, New Yrok: Unipublishers, 1981.
Walsh, Maurice N.	*War and the Human Race*, New York: Elsevier Publishing Company, 1971.
Walzer, Michael	*Just and Unjust Wars*, New York: Basic Books, 1977.

What Is a War Crime?

"The essence of war may be an expression of lawlessness, but surely it does not obviate the need for basic human decencies . . . obedience to basic laws of God and man."

War Must Be Governed by Laws

D. G. Kehl

D. G. Kehl frequently lectures on American literature and theology and is the author of several books. His view of the amorality of war stems from his belief that, although war may indeed be hell, such a fact does not negate the need to observe basic human decencies. Dr. Kehl is a chairman in the National Committee on Public Double Speak, an organization concerned with language manipulation, especially in the government.

As you read, consider the following questions:

1. For what crimes were Breaker Morant and his associates being tried?
2. On what grounds does the defense attempt to justify the actions of the accused?
3. What is the author's principle argument?
4. Do you agree with the author? Why or why not?

"Breaker Morant and the Ethics of War" by K.G. Kehl, April 23, 1982. Copyright by CHRISTIANITY TODAY 1982 and used by permission.

Moral and ethical issues have seldom been so vividly and forcefully dramatized as they have in the distinguished Australian film *Breaker Morant,* winner of 10 Academy Awards. Based on a play by Kenneth Ross, the film deals with the court martial of three Australian soldiers accused of killing six prisoners and a German missionary during the Boer War in South Africa (1899-1902). The defendants are Captain Harry "Breaker" Morant (former horsebreaker in Australia) — poet, singer, and Renaissance figure but volatile and impulsive; Lieutenant Peter Handcock — freewheeling ladies man; and George Witton — a sensitive but naive young lad.

Flashbacks reveal that when a contingent of their men was ambushed and their commanding officer, Captain Hunt, was killed and mutilated, Morant sought revenge by pursuing the Boers responsible and ordering them shot. Subsequently, Handcock shot a German missionary suspected of leading the Australians into the ambush, and Witton killed a Boer who jumped him and attempted to escape. All three defendants pleaded innocent on the grounds that they were following orders to execute prisoners, allegedly given by Captain Hunt, who, in turn, was allegedly following orders from supreme commander Lord Kitchener.

Rules of War

The basic issue can be stated as follows: Is it morally permissible to kill prisoners and even noncombatants in wartime? Relevant moral laws and principles include, most obviously, the Sixth Commandment — respect for human life. Also applicable are the words of Jesus labeled "The Golden Rule." Further, there are the man-made codes of warfare, especially those established by the Geneva Convention, which include such provisions as the treatment and care of the wounded and sick, humane treatment of prisoners, and protection of civilians and noncombatants in times of war.

In some ways paralleling the more recent Calley trial in the U.S., the case of Breaker Morant brings out at least five major points of supposed justification for violating the laws of God and man in killing prisoners and even civilians in wartime. Of primary significance in the defense's case is the argument of justification by precedent and authority of command. The defense attorney points out that "orders one would consider barbarous have already been issued: burning Boer farmhouses, herding women and children. . . ."

Herein, of course, is a basic conflict of principles. On the one hand, one is to obey the laws of God and men in regard to treating prisoners and noncombatants humanely. But on the other hand, one is to "obey them that have rule over [him], and submit [oneself]" (Heb. 13:17). Morant's initial response to Hunt's order, like Witton's response to Morant's, reveals the struggle.

A second justification is the argument of pragmatism, an appeal to survival. The rational goes: We are only reacting to the enemy's barbarous actions. Morant puts it bluntly: "We caught them and we shot them under Rule 303. We fought the Boer the way he fought us."

Similarly, Handcock demonstrates the explosive shells used by the Boers and says Witton: "These are dum-dums. They put a little hole here [indicating the forehead] and then in the back of the head—BOOM! Don't talk to *me* about right and wrong!"

The defense attorney expressed the point as follows: "When the rules and customs of war are departed from by one side, one must expect some departure from the other side. . . ." The pragmatic principle is essentially a reversal of the Golden Rule: "As thy enemy doeth unto thee, do ye even so unto him," or, "Do thy enemy in before he can do thee in."

Good Guys—Bad Guys

A third justification involves the *ad hominem* argument. Says the defense attorney: "The Boers are outlaws, renegades." The implication is that one is perfectly justified in killing prisoners and civilians because the enemy is morally inferior and therefore not worthy to live. War, in fact any kind of conflict, invariably involves stereotyping, false categorizing ("good guys" vs. "bad guys"), and dehumanization. In his classic treatise *On War*, Karl von Clausewitz defined war as "an act of violence intended to compel our opponent to fulfill our will." What is fundamental about violence is that the basic right of the dignity of human personhood is violated. Even before physical violence is done to him, psychological violence is done in that his right to dignity is violated when he is considered morally or ethnically inferior, and so unfit to live.

A fourth justification carries a double-edged argument: either it is a "just war" (justifiable?) in which the Almighty works his divine will through killing, or it is an ignoble cause, in which the means can hardly be expected to be noble—the end vilifies the means. Both angles are represented in Breaker Morant. The British chaplain's prayer implies the former: "Bless our men, O God, Who works His will in war as in peace." Morant expresses the other: "The Boer War is a bad cause: a few million men fighting against a few thousand farmers."

In neither case — whether a justifiable war or an unjustifiable one — are assaults on noncombatants justified. Paul Ramsey expressed the point well: "If combatants may and should be resisted directly by violent means to secure a desired and desirable victory, this also requires that noncombatants be never directly assaulted even to that same end" (*The Just War: Force and Political Responsibility*).

Finally, and perhaps most basic, is that justification predicated on the argument of the amorality of war. "Laws designed to moderate behavior in war may be made," Peter Craigie points out, "but it is of the essence of war to be an expression of lawlessness" (*The Problem of War in the Old Testament*). As his-

The Churchman, June/July, 1983. Reprinted with permission.

tory has amply illustrated, both sides commit "war crimes" — but ordinarily only the losers are brought to trial. Or, in the case of Breaker Morant, the individuals are sacrificed for "peace" as scapegoats.

War Is War

Morant clearly verbalizes the view of the amorality of war: "This is a war — not a debutante's ball! There are no rules here!" We have gone from the "ought" and the "ought not" to the *nought*. "It's a new kind of war for a new century," says Morant the improbable prophet.

The defense attorney argues that war alters human nature: "There is no evidence that Morant has an intrinsically barbarous nature. War changes men's nature. The barbarities of war are seldom conducted by barbarous men. The tragedies of war — they are conducted by normal men in abnormal situations." The agrument sounds convincing, but it is basically specious. The truth of the matter is that war is an objectification and extension of what is already within us. . . .

The essence of war may be an expression of lawlessness, but surely it does not obviate the need for basic human decencies, respect for human personhood, obedience to basic laws of God and man. The law of love is not rescinded on the field of battle. When we are breakers of this law we demean life — and we violate ourselves.

"It is the avowed purpose of the Army to make killers of all of you."

War Is Kill or Be Killed

Lesley J. McNair

Lieutenant General Lesley J. McNair was Commanding General of the U.S. Army Ground Forces when he delivered the following speech to his troops on November 11, 1942. It was Armistice Day and American soldiers had by then been fighting World War II for nearly a year. The following viewpoint is an excerpt from that speech. In it, General McNair clearly states that since the purpose of war is to conquer or be conquered, soldiers must virtually be prepared to become blind killing machines.

As you read, consider the following questions:

1. According to the author, why is the death of the three American soldiers in WWI of "special appeal?"
2. The author mentions certain surveys related to the willingness of American soldiers to fight. What were the results of these surveys?
3. Do you agree with the author? Why or why not?

Excerpted from an address to Troops of the Army Ground Forces over Blue Network from Washington, DC, November 11, 1942.

As a nation, we are just beginning to fight. Amid such events, I am thinking not so much of the Armistice Day that we have observed for so many years, but of another day close by— November 3, 1917—not 1918—25 years ago. On that day, three American soldiers died on the battlefields of France—our first battle deaths in that war. The drama enacted then carries special appeal today.

At that time, the 1st American Division—very green—was serving at the battle front on what might be called an instructional tour. The division was parceled out among the French troops, generally by battalion, under the French high command. A particular battalion of infantry had gone into line for the first time during the night of November 2-3. At about three o'clock in the morning, the Germans delivered a terrific artillery bombardment on a certain point of the line held by this battalion, smothering the trenches and pinning down the defenders. The fire was followed quickly by the German infantry in the assault, and in a short time the enemy was in the American trenches. The Germans withdrew at once, taking with them an American sergeant and ten privates as prisoners, which was the purpose of the raid. Three American soldiers were left dead in the trench.

The funeral was at the nearby French town of Bathelement, war-wrecked and within sound of the guns. The French general, under whose command the Americans were serving, spoke as follows:

"The death of this humble corporal and these privates appeals to us with unwonted grandeur. We will ask, therefore, that the mortal remains of these young men be left with us forever. We will inscribe upon their tombs, 'Here lie the first soldiers of the United States to fall on the fields of France for justice and liberty.' The passerby will stop and uncover his head. The travelers of France, of the Allied countries, of America, and the men of heart, who will come to visit our battlefields of Lorraine, will go out of their way to come here to bring to these graves the tribute of their respect and gratitude. Corporal Gresham, Private Enright, and Private Hay, in the name of France, I thank you. God receive your souls."

Thus we have the picture of war-hardened enemies pouncing on green American troops, taking every possible advantage of our lack of training and battle experience. Pearl Harbor was another such case.

Looking Ahead

It is fitting from a sentimental viewpoint that we memorialize today those who already have lost their lives in this war, and that we hail our fighting Allies who have borne and are bearing the burden while we train and cross the seas. But it is more practical and realistic to take stock of the situation ahead of us, and ask ourselves what we are going to do about it. Just how are we American soldiers going to do our part in crushing our enemies and winning the war? . . .

Our soldiers must have the fighting spirit. If you call that hating our enemies, then we must hate with every fiber of our being. We must lust for battle; our object in life must be to kill; we must scheme and plan night and day to kill. There need be no pangs of conscience, for our enemies have lighted the way to faster, surer, and crueler killing; they are past masters. We must hurry to catch up with them if we are to survive. Since killing is the object of our efforts, the sooner we get in the killing mood, the better and more skillful we shall be when the real test comes. The struggle is for survival—kill or be killed.

Modern warfare employs many deadly weapons, but men survive in spite of them. The one positive method is hand-to-hand combat. War kills by fire so far as possible, but final victory against a determined enemy is by close combat. For this reason, a fighting army is set to kill, and seeks ever to come to grips with the enemy.

I wonder whether you all are thinking in terms of killing by battling man to man. I do not know, and perhaps you yourself do not know your own feelings. A recent group of voluntary enlistments—totalling 30,000—reveals but five per cent for the infantry and armored force both. These two arms are preeminently those of close combat. Does this figure mean that our soldiers prefer the more genteel forms of warfare? If so, the sooner we change such preferences, the better for our Country. There is no doubt that Americans can and will fight when aroused they are brave in battle. You are going to get killing mad eventually; why not now, while you have time to learn throughly the art of killing. Soldiers learn quickly and well in battle—no doubt about that—but the method is costly to both you and the Nation.

Learn to Kill

Certain surveys have given the answer—true or false—that one-fourth of you want to fight, that one-fourth do not want to fight, and that one-half are on the fence. I'd prefer to think that

110

more than one-fourth want to fight; but, even if the figures are true, the picture is all right, because those of you who do not hate now are going to do so later. It is the avowed purpose of the Army to make killers of all of you; if not at home, far from the enemy, then overseas.

Also, there are certain indications that one-half of you in combat divisions expect to fight. All of you must not only expect to fight, but must be determined to fight and kill.

Again, it is said that one-half of you expect the war to end within two years. But your reason must tell you that it will end only when you finish it. If you intend to do the job in two years, make yourself into fighting devils now, not later.

Necessity vs. Morality

People should not allow their natural horror at the effects of unfamiliar weapons of war or certain acts on the periphery of war to blind them to the inherent horror of what the military apologist calls "legitimate" war. All war is horrendous; and it knows no moral law. Nations at war do not consult the moral code. They consult only the code of necessity. They do not act morally. They do not even act humanly. War compels them to act on a subhuman level, where only the law of necessity operates.

The Christian Century, August 18, 1943, p. 936.

If I seem to ask more of you tonight than you have given already, it is not that I do not appreciate what you have done and are doing. You have come a long way, and have earned the respect and gratitude of our people. But you still have a rough road to travel. It is too much to expect a peace loving nation such as ours to turn in a flash and in full fury to an all-out war overseas. Time is necessary for our people and our soldiers to make this fiendish transformation. I am not impatient with either you or our people. Nevertheless we must hurry—you soldiers of the Nation above all must hurry, for yours is the greatest burden and the gravest responsibility. You have the furthest to go. You must hit harder and harder. You must become tougher and tougher. You must hate more and more. Your devotion to duty must deepen. You must ration your pleasure time. You must think and act war. Casualty lists—and even a defeat perchance—must only fire your zeal the more. You must hurry and you must hate if you will do the job before you.

111

"The American crime of dropping atomic bombs on two Japanese cities is without parallel in world history."

Hiroshima Was a War Crime

Shigetoshi Iwamatsu

Shigetoshi Iwamatsu is a survivor of the 1945 bombing of Nagasaki. Currently he is a professor in the faculty of economics at Nagasaki University. In the following viewpoint, Professor Iwamatsu analyzes the historical events leading up to the bombings, comparing them with international nuclear politics today.

As you read, consider the following questions:

1. What was the author's immediate reaction to the bombing of Nagasaki?
2. Does the author blame America alone for war crimes? Explain your answer.
3. According to the author, what factors contributed to the use of the atomic bomb?
4. According to the author, why did the Japanese decide to surrender?

"A Perspective on the War Crimes" by Shigetoshi Iwamatsu, February 1982. Reprinted by permission of THE BULLETIN OF THE ATOMIC SCIENTISTS, a magazine of science and public affairs. Copyright © 1982 by the Educational Foundation for Nuclear Science, Chicago, Ill., 60637.

Victims of the atomic bombs dropped on Hiroshima and Nagasaki emphasize, quite naturally, the perculiarly brutal effects of nuclear weapons, which are far beyond comparison with the effects of any other weapons. They are right in calling for the elimination of all weapons, particularly nuclear, because they have experienced their merciless cruelty.

An Eyewitness Account

I, myself, suffered from the atomic bomb in Nagasaki on August 9, 1945. Since then, having reflected upon my own experience, I have been appealing continuously to the world for an understanding of the effects of nuclear weapons and for eliminating nuclear arms and energy from the world.

I was a student at the time of the burning of Hiroshima and Nagasaki. To assist the war effort, all students in Japan worked in factories except those who went to the battlefield. My own work was at the Mitsubishi Ordinance Factory making torpedoes for Japanese military use.

After the bombing of Hiroshima, Japanese military headquarters announced that the city had suffered slight damage; nothing very serious. But on the morning of August 9, when I was at the torpedo factory, there was an air-raid warning. A few American planes flew over without dropping bombs and soon the "all clear" signal sounded. We went back to the factory, but later, at 11:02 a.m., I saw an extremely bright flash of light through the window.

At that moment, there was only time to think: What happened? Electrical trouble? And then, all around me, the slate roof and walls, and the windows were smashed, with fragments flying everywhere. Many of the people in the factory were killed instantly or died that night or a few days later as a result of burns from heat rays, shock waves or radiation. The factory was located eight-tenths of a mile from the epicenter of the blast.

I ran from the site toward a northern suburb, fearing a second attack. The fence surrounding the factory as well as the houses nearby had been instantly destroyed. Many other survivors were also running in the same direction, under the strange, dark sky covered by the mushroom cloud generated by the atomic bomb blast.

The scene was like hell. Wounded people were running with torn-off skin hanging down like old rags, with bloodied heads and faces blackened from the blast.

About an hour later, in the garden of a doctor's house, I saw a nurse who had come from a nearby town to look after the people.

She was crying after she glanced at the sufferers, because she could not bear to look at the seriously wounded. Wanting to make my way to my home, I returned to a bridge near the factory, but the fire was still burning so fiercely that I could not get through. I decided to stay at a railway bridge, where I saw a lot of school girls who lay on the ground, with eyes shut and breathing faintly but without visible hurt. They must have died shortly thereafter because of the invisible radioactivity.

The Victims Remember

I remember feeling a tremendous sense of despair and hopelessness, thinking about the war and the fate of Japan. I thought very little about myself and the miracle that my life had been spared.

After several hours, I was carried to a city far from Nagasaki by the rescue train which came from the north and stopped some distance from Nagasaki station. I saw a lot of dead or dying victims laying on the floor of the train like hurt animals.

After spending the night in a hall of the primary school I returned by train and walked through the completely devastated streets of Nagasaki. I saw many charred corpses which, I believe, nobody could bear to look at. At this point I was exposed to a great quantity of induced radioactivity and nuclear fallout in addition to the instantaneous radioactivity at the time of explosion.

Since that time, those who suffered from the bombing have been earnestly appealing to the world to take heed of their pain, agony, bitter life, anger, rage, despair and sorrow. These appeals have been almost in vain. . . .

Whenever I lecture to my class about the atomic bombs which the United States dropped on two inhabited cities in Japan, I first illustrate various Japanese war crimes, before and during World War II, which are much more grave than was generally adjudged by the International Military Tribunal. This is because I believe that the suffering inflicted by the atomic bomb, however incredibly tragic that was, must be protested to the world only after Japanese war crimes have been severely criticized by the Japanese themselves.

My own historic field of vision is not shared by the majority of atomic bomb victims. They forget the people who were murdered, shot, tortured, enslaved, plundered, burned and violated by the ferocious Japanese imperialist army of the Tenno Emperor system. Only a minority remembers. . . .

114

Both Sides Guilty

Japanese war crimes are not effaced by the bitter aftermath of the atomic bombing, even though the devastation might be termed genocide and the resulting diseases of the sufferers are incurable forever. Japanese crimes were another type of genocide, which can be atoned for only by Japanese efforts toward peace and international friendship.

What can we learn from all of this? The American crime of dropping atomic bombs on two Japanese cities is without parallel in world history. But the imperialist Japanese attacks on Korea, China, Southeast Asia, the United States, the United Kingdom and Holland were extremely serious war crimes, which cannot be nullified by the U.S. crime of dropping atomic bombs.

A Day to Remember

It was the most important day in the history of warfare, international relations, radiation biology, trauma, and man's inhumanity to man. A fearsome, indelible day of destiny.

George D. Lundberg, *The Journal of the American Medical Association*, August 5, 1983.

But the U.S. crime is not nullified because of previous Japanese war crimes. Americans have guilt to bear even though the Japanese committed serious war crimes. The war crimes of both countries do not cancel each other out. The only right approach is to judge by criteria composed of humanistic, social, international and global viewpoints. According to this method, it must be concluded that Japanese aggression and atrocities were serious crimes and, at the same time, the American dropping of the atomic bombs was a grave outrage. Each nation should consider its own crimes, apologize to each other, atone, and try to build a peaceful world through new and higher steps. . . .

The brutal mass murder and destruction wrought by atomic bombs at Hiroshima and Nagasaki has been underestimated. They have been labeled infants' toys compared with the far more powerful weapons in the world's expanding nuclear stockpile.

This underestimation has generated not only the low estimation of the meaning of the U.S. atomic bombing of Japan, but also the opinion that the nuclear arms race is necessary as a deterrent.

But in truth, use of atomic bombs was the supreme offense

against humanity which must not be repeated. I know this not only because of my own experience but also because of what I can see of the political, military, racial and other factors that contributed to the dropping of bombs:

● The United States dropped the genocide weapons on Hiroshima and Nagasaki, even though there was no need to do so. President Truman's explanation was only an awkward excuse. By that time Japan's war potential had decreased to a minimum. It had practically no defending force left.

● The United States decided to use the atomic bombs not on Germany but on Japan in the autumn of 1944, when the Allies already knew the surrender of both Japan and Germany was imminent. The selection of Japan might well have been motivated by the racism which regards the yellow Asian with contempt.

● The United States raced to complete the bombs as soon as possible—before the Japanese could surrender, which would have been in the near future. The rush to complete the bombs was not to achieve Japanese submission but for another aim.

An Unnecessary Deed

What was this aim? In choosing the cities upon which the bombs were to be dropped, U.S. authorities preferred those with many munitions factories and laborers, but no defense forces. Tokyo, where the Tenno, the political and military leaders lived, and Kyoto, a traditional city, were excluded. The majority of the laborers had been drafted for active military service during the war, and the people who were working in the factories were old farmers, tradespeople or office workers, women and young students. There were also Koreans, who had been violently taken from their homeland, and prisoners of war. There were many houses and schools surrounding the factories. Most of the people who were killed or injured by the genocide weapons were not soldiers but civilians—the elderly, women and children, Koreans and unarmed prisoners.

The atomic bombing did not aim at—nor did it bring about—Japanese submission. The Tenno and other Japanese top leaders decided to surrender not because Hiroshima and Nagasaki were destroyed but because of Soviet entry into the Pacific war on August 8.

The devastation of two cities did not cause Japan's top leaders to surrender to the Allies because they did not care that much about the people's distress and sorrow. Because they cherished the Tenno system Soviet participation was the largest and final shock to them. They discussed the "enemy's" guarantee that the Japanese could retain the Tenno system. This was the deciding factor.

• Atomic bombs were the product of the energetic collaboration of eminent scientists, including many Nobel Prize winners. In Japan, an example of collaboration of scientists to devise cruel weapons is that of Ishii's group, which worked on biological weapons. But the military-university-industrial complex was established in the United States after the Manhattan Project.

• The United States occupation policy in Japan should be seen as an extension of the brutality of the atomic bombing. The United States suppressed freedom of discussion, speech and writing, especially on the part of atomic bomb survivors. They could not relate their own experience and appeal against further fission explosions. Letters and newspapers were checked for a time. U.S. authorities prohibited publication of the experience of survivors and the photographing of the devastation.

Cameramen of the Japan Cinema Company, working in collaboration with the academic investigation team sponsored by the Education Ministry of Japan, were captured in Nagasaki by the U.S. Military Police on October 17, 1945. All members of the camera team were forced to return to Tokyo and were confined in a room of the building that served as American military General Headquarters. There they edited their films of the devastated Hiroshima and Nagasaki. Those films were then all sent to the U.S. Army. But the camera team dared to make a secret copy, at the risk of death, for the future use of the Japanese people.

"Experience whispers that the pity is not that we used the bomb to end the Japanese war but that it wasn't ready earlier to end the German one."

Hiroshima Was Not a War Crime

Paul Fussell

During World War II, Paul Fussell, recipient of a Bronze Star and two Purple Hearts, was assigned to prepare for "Operation Olympic," the invasion of Japan. After the war, he entered Pomona College as a literature major and achieved a Ph.D. from Harvard University. Mr. Fussell is currently Donald T. Regan Professor of English Literature at the University of Pennsylvania. In the following viewpoint, he explains why the atomic bombing of Hiroshima was not the criminal act many have portrayed it to be. He argues, in fact, that it saved the adversaries from casualties that would have numbered in the millions.

As you read, consider the following questions:

1. What were the arguments offered by Joesph Alsop and David Joravsky regarding the atomic bombings of Japan?
2. What were some examples of Japanese and American "savagery" during WWII, according to the author?
3. According to the author, what would the cost have been in American lives if Japan were invaded?
4. Has this viewpoint changed your opinion of the Hiroshima–Nagasaki bombings? Explain your answer.

"Hiroshima: A Soldier's View," August 22 & 29, 1981 by Paul Fussell. Reprinted by permission of THE NEW REPUBLIC, © 1981 The New Republic, Inc.

Many years ago in New York I saw on the side of a bus a whis-key ad which I've remembered all this time, for it's been for me a model of the brief poem. Indeed, I've come upon few short poems subsequently that evinced more genuine poetic talent. The ad consisted of two lines of "free verse," thus:

In life, experience is the great teacher.
In Scotch, Teacher's is the great experience.

For present purposes we can jettison the second line (licking our lips ruefully as it disappears), leaving the first to encapsulate a principle whose banality suggests that it enshrines a most use-ful truth. I bring up the matter this August, the 36th anniversary of the A-bombing of Hiroshima and Nagasaki, to focus on some-thing suggested by the long debate about the ethics, if any, of that affair: namely, the importance of experience, sheer vulgar experience, in influencing, if not determining, one's views about the first use of the bomb. And the experience I'm talking about is that of having come to grips, face to face, with an enemy who designs your death. The experience is common to those in the infantry and the Marines and even the line Navy, to those, in short, who fought the Second World war mindful always that their mission was, as they were repeatedly told, "to close with the enemy and destroy him." I think there's something to be learned about the war, as well as about the tendency of historical memory unwittingly to resolve ambiguity, by considering some of the ways testimonies emanating from experience complicate attitudes about the cruel ending of that cruel war. . . .

Two Familiar Arguments

In an interesting exchange last year in the *New York Review of Books,* Joseph Alsop and David Joravsky set forth the by now familiar arguments on both sides of the debate. You'll be able to guess which sides they chose once you know that Alsop experienced capture by the Japanese at Hong Kong in 1942 and that Joravsky made no mortal contact with the Japanese: a young soldier, he was on his way to the Pacific when the war ended. The editors of the *New York Review* have given their debate the tendentious title "Was the Hiroshima Bomb Necessary?" — surely an unanswerable question (unlike "Was It Effective?") and one suggesting the intellectual difficulties involved in imposing *ex post facto* a rational ethics on this event. Alsop focuses on the power and fanaticism of War Minis-ter Anami, who insisted that Japan fight to the bitter end, defending the main islands with the same means and tenacity with which it had defended Iwo and Okinawa. He concludes:

"Japanese surrender could never have been obtained, at any rate without the honor-satisfying bloodbath envisioned by . . . Anami, if the hideous destruction of Hiroshima and Nagasaki had not finally galvanized the peace advocates into tearing up the entire Japanese book of rules." The Japanese planned to deploy the undefeated bulk of their ground forces, over two million men, plus 10,000 kamikaze planes, in a suicidal defense. That fact, says Alsop, makes it absurd to "hold the common view, by now hardly challenged by anyone, that the decision to drop the two bombs on Japan was wicked in itself, and that President Truman and all others who joined in making or who [like Oppenheimer] assented to this decision shared in the wickedness." And in explanation of "the two bombs" Alsop adds: "The true, climactic, and successful effort of the Japanese peace advocates . . . did not begin in deadly earnest until *after* the second bomb had destroyed Nagasaki. The Nagasaki bomb was thus the trigger to all the developments that led to peace."

Paul Fussell

Joravsky, now a professor of history at Northwestern, argues on the other hand that those who decided to use the bomb on cities betray defects of "reason and self-restraint." It all needn't have happened, he asserts, "if the US government had been willing to take a few more days and to be a bit more thoughtful in opening the age of nuclear warfare." But of course in its view it wasn't doing that: that's a historian's tidy hindsight. The government was ending the war conclusively, as well as irrationally remembering Pearl Harbor with a vengeance. It didn't know then what everyone knows now about leukemia and carcinoma and birth defects. . . .

Lest We Forget

The Alsop-Joravsky debate, which can be seen as reducing finally to a collision between experience and theory, was conducted with a certain civilized respect for evidence. Not so the way the new scurrilous agitprop *New Statesman* conceives those favoring the bomb and those opposing. They are, on the one hand, says Bruce Page, "the imperialist class-forces acting through Harry Truman," and, on the other, those representing "the humane, democratic virtues" — in short, "fascists" opposed to "populists." But ironically the bomb saved the lives not of any imperialists but only of the low and humble, the quintessentially democratic huddled masses — the conscripted enlisted men man-

---

It Saved Lives

Those who feel the Hiroshima and Nagasaki victims — survivors — suffered longer and more painfully than other living targets may not have seen some of the other human wreckage war left. This is not to say that the agonies of the A-bomb victims were not truly horrible. They were. But those two major bombings a person can point at as being strategically decisive. And in the end, to repeat, they saved lives. Perhaps a million or more. You sometimes wonder about other matters of strategy, but not this.

William Sumner, *St. Paul Pioneer Press*, August 7, 1983.

---

ning the fated invasion divisions. Bruce Page was nine years old when the war ended. For a man of that experience, phrases like "imperialist class forces" come easily, and the issues look perfectly clear.

He's not the ony one to have forgotten, if he ever knew, the savagery of the Pacific war. The dramatic postwar Japanese success at hustling and merchandising and tourism has (happily, in many ways) effaced foremost people important elements of the assault context in which Hiroshima should be viewed. It is easy to forget what Japan was like before it was first destroyed and then humiliated, tamed, and constitutionalized by the West. "Implacable, treacherous, barbaric"—those were Admiral Halsey's characterizations of the enemy, and at the time few facing the Japanese would deny that they fit to a T. One remembers the captured American airmen locked for years in packing-crates, the prisoners decapitated, the gleeful use of bayonets on civilians. The degree to which Americans register shock and extraordinary shame about the Hiroshima bomb correlates closely with lack of information about the war.

And the savagery was not just on one side. There was much sadism and brutality—undeniably racist—on ours. No Marine was fully persuaded of his manly adequacy who didn't have a well-washed Japanese skull to caress and who didn't have a go at treating surrendering Japs as rifle targets. Herman Wouk remembers it correctly while analyzing Ensign Keith in *The Caine Mutiny:* "Like most of the naval executioners of Kwajalein, he seems to regard the enemy as a species of animal pest." And the enemy felt the same way about us: "From the grim and desperate taciturnity with which the Japanese died, they seemed on their side to believe they were contending with an invasion of large armed ants." Hiroshima seems to follow in natural sequence: "This obliviousness on both sides to the fact that the opponents were human beings may perhaps be cited as the key to the many massacres of the Pacific war." Since the Japanese resisted so madly, let's pour gasoline into their emplacements and light it and shoot the people afire who try to get out. Why not? Why not blow them all up? Why not, indeed drop a new kind of big bomb on them? Why allow one more American high school kid to see his intestines blown out of his body and spread before him in the dirt while he screams when we can end the whole thing just like that?

Casualties Were High

Onokinawa, only weeks before Hiroshima, 123,000 Japanese and Americans *killed* each other. "Just awful" was the comment not of some pacifist but of MacArthur. One million American casualties was his estimate of the cost of the forthcoming invasion. And that invasion was not just a hypothetical threat, as some theorists have argued. It was genuinely in train, as I know because I was to be in it. When the bomb ended the war I was in the 45th Infantry Division, which had been through the European war to the degree that it had needed to be reconstituted two or three times. We were in a staging area near Reims, ready to be shipped across the United States for final preparation in the Philippines. My division was to take part in the invasion of Honshu in March 1946. (The earlier invasion of Kyushu was to be carried out by 700,000 infantry already in the Pacific.) I was a 21-year-old second lieutenant leading a rifle platoon. Although still officially in one piece, in the German war I had already been wounded in the leg and back severely enough to be adjudged, after the war, 40 percent disabled. But even if my legs buckled whenever I jumped out of the back of the truck, my condition was held to be satisfactory for whatever lay ahead. When the bombs dropped and news began to circulate that "Operation Olympic" would not, after all, take place, that we would not be

---

The Bomb Saved Japan

The atomic bomb was the result of scientists of America making efforts to develop industry and new sources of energy. It was most regrettable that the bomb was used for war. The military had driven Japan to a stage that if it could not win, it would not surrender. It surely would have lost the war and many people would have starved if the atom bomb had not been dropped. When one considers the possibility that the Japanese military would have sacrificed the entire nation if it were not for the atomic bomb attack, then this bomb might be described as having saved Japan.

Taro Takemi, "Remembrances of the War and the Bomb," *The Journal of the American Medical Association*, August 5, 1983.

---

obliged to run up the beaches near Tokyo assault-firing while being mortared and shelled, for all the fake manliness of our facades we cried with relief and joy. We were going to live. We were going to grow up to adulthood after all. When the *Enola Gay* dropped its package, "There were cheers," says John Toland, "over the intercom; it meant the end of the war.". . .

Experience whispers that the pity is not that we used the bomb to end the Japanese war but that it wasn't ready earlier to end the German one. If only it could have been rushed into production faster and dropped at the right moment on the Reich chancellery or Berchtesgaden or Hitler's military headquarters in East Prussia or—Wagnerian *coup de theatre*—at Rommel's phony state funeral, most of the Nazi hierarchy could have been pulverized immediately, saving not just the embarrassment of the Nuremburg trials but the lives of about four million Jews,

Poles, Slavs, gypsies, and other "subhumans," not to mention the lives and limbs of millions of Allied and Axis soldiers. If the bomb could have been ready even as late as July 1944, it could have reinforced the Von Stauffenberg plot and ended the war then and there. If the bomb had only been ready in time, the men of my infantry platoon would not have been killed and maimed.

"Lt. William L. Calley is not innocent, but his superiors' guilt is black."

Mylai Was a War Crime

Arnold Toynbee

Arnold Toynbee's original and bold approach to world history contributed to his popularity as a scholar of ancient history who viewed the Western world from the outside. Born in London in 1889, he is famous for his critically acclaimed twelve-volume *A Study of History* which set a standard for historical writing for many contemporary historians. Until his death in 1975, Mr. Toynbee lectured extensively and wrote countless essays for publication, including the following viewpoint which appeared in the *Observer*, London, England. In it, he explains why he believes that the Mylai incident was a war crime for which he lays final blame on Calley's superiors.

As you read, consider the following questions:

1. Why does the author believe that all war is a crime?
2. According to the author, when did our present laws of war originate?
3. According to the author, with whom does the final blame for Mylai lie?
4. Do you agree with the author? Why or why not?

Originally appeared in *The Observer*, London, England, 1971. Reprinted with permission.

The conviction of Lt. William L. Calley for military atrocities against civilians in a war zone, and President Nixon's intervention to release him from imprisonment concern not only Americans, but all of us. Calley is unquestionably a murderer according to the "laws of war" that, since the 18th Century, have been accepted by all "civilized" states and have been written by each of them into its own military regulations.

But are there mitigating considerations? Is their guilt, both legal and moral, actually greater than Calley's? If it is, how far up the hierarchy does the tide of guilt rise? Gen. William C. Westmoreland has hastened to disclaim responsibility. If he is guiltless, does the buck stop somewhere below him, or does it pass over his head up to the Commander-in-Chief, who, in the United States, is the President?

War itself is a crime. Throughout the history of this criminal institution it has always been recognized that war needed justification. A "just war" (actually a contradiction in terms) must be a war that is being waged for self-defense, or for the vindication of rights if all non-violent means of redress have failed, or in fulfillment of an obligation to spread the right faith, or to stop the spreading of the wrong faith.

This last "justification," which is the Americans ground for waging a holy war against communism in Vietnam, comes close to the sactioning of unprovoked aggressive war, and no one has had the face to admit to this (no, not even Ghengis Khan or the Spanish Conquistadores; Ghengis Khan invoked heaven's command, and the Conquistadores asserted their king's sovereign rights).

War is a crime because it is against nature to kill members of one's own species. Even capital punishment for a convicted murderer is questionable. Killing an "enemy" soldier in war is so unnatural that human beings have to be dehumanized in order to turn them into soldiers. They have to be "conditioned" by rigid discipline and by hypnotizing drill to break the built-in taboo "thou shalt not kill." But when once this taboo has been broken it is difficult to set limits to the breach of it by confining the killing to "enemy" soldiers.

Historical Examples

If the civilian population of an invaded country, or even only some unidentifiable portion of it is known by the invading army. to be hostile, the invading troops will live in fear of unforeseeable attack by civilians in plain clothes, and this is the psychological situation in which military atrocities against civilians are likely to be committed. Cases in point, besides the U.S. Army now intervening in South Vietnam, in an American-made Vietnamese civil war, are the German Army in Belgium in 1914 and the British "black and tans" in Ireland after World War I.

Conditioning: This is done to the soldier by officers and by the government by whom these officers are commissioned. Invasion: This is an act of state. It is not true that offenses are inevitable when the offenses in question are wars. But, all the more, woe to that man by whom the offense cometh. The originator of the offense is eminently guilty when the offense is one which need not have been, and ought not have been, committed. Here is the moral issue that has been raised by the conviction of Lt. Calley, and this issue is likely to be followed up in the trial of Capt. Ernest Medina.

Responsibility of Superiors

The effectiveness of the law of war depends, above all else, on holding those in command and in policy-making positions responsible for rank-and-file behavior on the field of battle. The reports of neuropsychiatrists, trained in combat therapy, have suggested that unrestrained troop behavior is almost always tacitly authorized by commanding officers — at least to the extent of conveying the impression that outrageous acts will not be punished. It would thus be a deception to punish the trigger men at [Mylai] without also looking higher on the chain of command for the real source of responsibility.

Richard A. Falk, "The Circle of Responsibility," *The Nation*, January 26, 1970.

Our present "laws of war" originated in a moral reaction against the atrocities committed in the 15th Century and the 17th Century western "wars of religion," in which war had been waged indiscriminately against entire populations. Since the 18th Century, governments have tried to reduce war to a game played with "living chessmen," i.e., paid professional soldiers in uniform. The intention has been to exempt civilians from being massacred, raped and robbed by the troops. Civilians are supposed to be immune, so long as they remain non-combatant.

In the 18th Century this mitigation of the horrors of war was more or less effective, except for the license to sack fortified cities taken by storm after the military command had rejected the option of capitulating. The last bad case of this particular atrocity was the sacking of Badajoz by British Troops in 1812. The victims were not the French garrison; they were the Spanish civilain inhabitants whom the British troops were supposed to be liberating. In 1812, Spain was Britain's Vietnam.

Persons subject to law are deemed to know what the law is, and are found guilty if they have disobeyed it. Soldiers' are supposed to be instructed in the laws of war, and they are required to abide by the laws of war, even if they have been given military orders to break them. The laws override the orders; illegal orders have to be disobeyed.

This is an agonizing responsibility. It aggravates the agony of active military service, which is already more than human nature can bear. But there is no way out. The laws of war become a dead letter if this legal and moral responsibility is not laid upon every soldier, whatever his rank.

But this necessary rule does accentuate the legal and moral responsibility of a soldier's superiors in the chain of command. Have they instructed the soldier fully and clearly? Have they made sure that he has understood their instructions? Have they tested his fitness for carrying out the military duties that have been assigned to him?

'A CADET WILL NOT LIE, CHEAT OR STEAL, OR TOLERATE THOSE WHO DO'

Reprinted with permission from the *Minneapolis Star and Tribune.*

The Real Criminals

Lt. Calley seems not to have been properly instructed. He may have been intellectually incapable of understanding what his duty was in conflict between the laws of war, embodied in standing military regulations, and ad hoc order. He was certainly unfit to be put in charge of the operation at My Lai. He is not guiltless. Even if his intellect was inadequate, his feelings ought not to have been. Some of the soldiers under his command abstained from taking part in the massacre, in defiance of his orders.

In Algeria, the French conscripts revolted against their professional officers' monstrously unprofessional orders to commit atrocities, and the conscripts' human indignation and moral courage enabled President Charles de Gaulle to stop that war.

American conscripts in Vietnam have no excuse for falling below French conscripts' standards in Algeria. Calley is not innocent, but his superiors' guilt is black. "Search and destroy." "Free fire zone." Are these mere slogans, or are they general directives, or are they positive orders? Whatever they are, they are incitements to genocide. If the American people are to recover their self-respect, the search — not for Viet Cong, but for American war criminals — will have to be carried further and higher.

"Instead of finding cold-blooded killers among the former members of Charlie Company, I found stunned, dazed, guilt-ridden boys."

Mylai Was Not a War Crime

Martin Gershen

Martin Gershen is a veteran news reporter who won the Ernie Pyle award while reporting in Vietnam for the North American Newspaper Alliance. He is a recipient of the Page One Award from the American Newspaper Guild for his series "Why Mylai?" In the following viewpoint, Mr. Gershen explains why he believes that Mylai was not a war crime. Instead he found the incident to be the result of a group of frightened boys reacting to frightening circumstances.

As you read, consider the following questions:

1. According to the author, what was the ethnic and racial composition of Charlie Company?
2. What does the author write about the situation in Mylai in the weeks and months before the killings?
3. Do you agree with the author? Why or why not?

Martin Gershen, "Where Do We Measure Mylai on the Scale of Viet Evil?" October 27, 1979. Reprinted with permission from *Human Events*.

To the careful reader, the stories out of Southeast Asia become more hair-raising as time goes by.

The reader must be attentive because the real horror stories are buried at the bottom of columns of print somewhere on the inside pages of newspapers.

One story, for example, tucked neatly away in the New York *Times* last July, reported that 85 Vietnamese refugees, more than half of them children, had been murdered by soldiers of the Hanoi regime on June 22.

The massacre occurred on an island claimed by four countries, but occupied by Vietnamese troops. The innocent civilians had been trying to flee their country when their leaky boat ran aground. Eight people survived the massacre and made it to the Philippines, where they told their story.

The story was limited to two paragraphs.

Then last August, a slightly longer story, buried in the Baltimore *Sun,* told of how 500 Vietnamese refugees were presumed drowned in a typhoon after their boat was pushed back to sea by fellow Asians.

According to some estimates, about one million Vietnamese, Cambodians and Laotians have fled their countries since the United States left Southeast Asia and the Communist regimes took over.

And the reports indicate that tens of thousands of refugees have died at sea. Those who make it to Indonesia, Malaysia or Thailand are raped, robbed or beaten before they are permitted to live under almost subhuman conditions.

The reason I've become so upset over these reports is that nobody is accusing anybody of racist murder. Jane Fonda has raised barely a peep over the brutal actions of her North Vietnamese friends.

Nor have we heard so much from the vociferous portion of the generation of the 1960s who claimed to be idealistically opposed to war, violence and bloodshed, and who so readily condemned the United States for being genocidal maniacs in Vietnam.

A Tragic Event

Nearly 12 years ago another tragic story came out of Vietnam, a story in which I became involved and which appeared on the front pages of the U.S. press for a year or more.

It was called the Mylai Massacre.

A company of infantrymen was accused of wiping out a village of innocent Vietnamese civilians. The antiwar faction in the United States, determined to prove that U.S. soldiers were

131

callous murderers while the North Vietnamese were peaceful civilians, sized upon the company as scapegoats. Twenty-five members of the company were courtmartialed. Only one, Lt. William L. Calley, was found guilty of the murder of 22 Vietnamese civilians.

I became involved as a newsman and traveled around the country and to Vietnam interviewing former members of the company, their relatives, Vietnamese, psychiatrists, anybody who could shed light on the tragedy.

My findings were not popularly received.

Instead of finding cold-blooded killers among the former members of the company, I found stunned, dazed guilt-ridden boys. Most of them had been reluctant draftees scooped from the ghettos, the farms, or the poor neighborhoods of working-class America. The reason they didn't act like professional killers was that they weren't.

At least two had been dragged into the Army by the FBI. One had changed his name twice to stay out of the Army. The average educational level of the company was somewhere between grammar school dropout and high school dropout.

Many had been unemployed or had worked at menial, unskilled jobs before entering the Army. An Army report in dicated the members of this hapless company "had less education and were less trainable than the average soldiers of that period."

Between 8 percent and 12 per cent of the company had below normal IQs, scoring between the 10th and the 30th percentile in the Armed Forces Qualifications Test. Army psychiatrists say anybody can score in the 20th percentile just by guessing at the answers. Psychiatrists who study war also say the higher a soldier's IQ and the more educated he is, the better infantryman he makes.

In other words, the kind of soldier the United States needed in Vietnam was the kind protesting the war, or going off to college, or Canada.

Members of Charlie Company complained to me that they never really knew what they were fighting for. Indoctrination never went beyond basic infantry training.

Ironically, the company had no racial problems. "We were all brothers," recalled one of its black members.

Minorities Involved

To the best of my calculations, between one-third and one-half of the company was black. The Army wouldn't say. There was a healthy representation of Mexican-Americans, Puerto Ricans and other Hispanics. There was also one Filipino, one Hawaiian, one American Indian and three South Vietnamese interpreters in the company. Two of its three rifle platoon sergeants were black. The third was Hispanic.

Capt. Ernest Lou Medina, the company commander, was a Mexican-American who came from a background of poverty, was intimately acquainted with prejudice and had risen by his own bootstraps from nothing to a promising young star in the Army's officer corps—until Mylai.

Yet, in the aftermath of Mylai, this company was accused of being racist, because the U.S. Army was accused of being racist, because the United States was accused of being racist, because Vietnamese were being killed.

Not Real Criminals

War is hell, and when we take a young man into the Army and train him to kill and train him to take orders and send him into a strange foreign land to follow the flag, and he then in the wild confusion of combat commits an act which, long after the event, is made the basis of a capital criminal charge, simple justice demands that he be treated fairly by the press, by his government and by the branch of the service in which he served.

J. Robert Elliott, U.S. District Court Judge, in a postscript to his decision reversing William L. Calley's conviction in the Mylai killings.

Ignored in all the debates was the fact that Quang Ngai Province, where Mylai was located, was a Vietcong stronghold from where Communist guerrillas always fought the Saigon government.

Mylai was known as "Pinkville" to the U.S. troops and the members of Charlie Company were afraid of this village. They had trouble everytime they came near Mylai during their patrols in the rice paddies of Quang Ngai Province. "We always got our ass tore trying to get to Pinkville," remembered Fred Widmer, a member of the company.

The company's first casualty was killed in Pinkville and its members feared the guerrillas known to be in the area.

Charlie Company suffered heavy casualties from the time it arrived in Vietnam in December 1967 until March 1968, when it was sent on its ill-fated assault on Mylai. It never received replacements until after the Mylai affair.

Its worst experience occurred on Feb. 25, 1968, a Sunday, just three weeks before Mylai, when the company was trapped in a minefield. Several of the most popular members of the company were killed. Many were wounded physically. All were wounded mentally, but the Army gives no Purple Hearts for wounds that don't draw blood.

Participants Remember

Michael Bernhardt, a member of the company, said, "The psychological effect of the minefield was more devastating than the physical effect."

Despite its casualties, the company had never once seen its enemy.

As many an infantry veteran would agree, there is nothing more devastating physically and psychologically than an encounter with a minefield—or an unseen guerrilla.

"The way to destroy the enemy is to destroy his moral," observed Robert Joel Van Leer, who had been Medina's radioman until he lost his leg in the minefield, and Charlie Company's morale was pretty much destroyed that Sunday.

Then it had its collective face rubbed in the dirt just two days before Mylai, when one of the best-liked members of the company, Sgt. George Cox, a father figure, was killed by a booby trap.

Richard Hendrickson, who survived the booby trap, remembered "just a greyness," when he awoke after the explosion.

"I didn't know until I woke up that I was blind. I asked the doctor would I see and he said no, no, it's permanent, and I broke up and cried."

Hendrickson also lost two legs, the use of one arm, a finger on his other hand and most of his hearing. He also was wounded in his genitals.

"If I tell you we lost 28 men wounded and four killed in that minefield that's not the same as you being there and watching us lose those people," Widmer told me as he tried to explain the psychological effect of the minefield.

"Hendrickson lost his arms, his legs, his sight and he's going deaf. I'd rather be dead than to come home decapped," he added.

The company was told it was going into Mylai with two other companies to get the guerrillas who had killed or wounded 42 of its members. The men were frightened, but they believed they would end the guerrilla harassment and avenge the death of their comrades and the atrocities committed on people like Hendrickson.

It was a frightened group of poorly trained, poorly led, psy-

134

chologically scarred draftees that stormed Mylai that tragic day in March 1968.

What happened afterward wasn't the same as North Vietnamese killing children in a leaky boat on an unnamed island. And it wasn't like pushing innocent men, women and children into the path of a typhoon.

One thing seems to be certain after witnessing what is happening to the boat people. The Communist cadres of Southeast Asia aren't the peace-loving idealists the antiwar movement in the United States claimed they were.

There was another story in the New York *Times* (August 13) in which veterans of the antiwar movement were interviewed nearly a dozen years later.

Said one woman, "Logic dictated you should be against the war. But I don't really know enough about history to argue intelligently. It's a problem I think a lot of us had and still do."

So maybe the country should apologize to Charlie Company. Or at least, in light of recent events in Southeast Asia, maybe the country should reserve opinion and welcome Charlie Company home. Or what is left of Charlie Company.

"Well-adjusted people may get caught up in a tangle of social forces that makes them goose-step their way toward . . . the calculated execution of six million Jews."

Could You Commit a War Crime?

Molly Harrower

Molly Harrower received her Ph.D. in experimental psychology from Smith College in 1934. A clinical psychologist, she is Professor Emeritus at the University of Florida and is editor of the American Lecture Series in Psychology, a position she has held since 1945. Dr. Harrower is the author of several works including *Psychodiagnostic Testing: An Empirical Approach* (1965) and *Kurt Kaffka: An Unwitting Self-Portrait.* In the following viewpoint, she focuses upon the mental status of leading Nazi war criminals. She concludes that for the most part they were not deranged individuals but well-adjusted and, in some cases, superior personalities.

As you read, consider the following questions:

1. What is the Rorschach test?
2. Who is Stanley Milgram? Describe his experiment.
3. According to the Rorschach test, how were some of the leading Nazis rated?
4. Do you agree with the author that ordinary, well-adjusted people are capable of commiting war crimes similar to those of the Nazis? Explain your answer.

Molly Harrower, "Were Hitler's Henchmen Mad?" July, 1976. REPRINTED FROM PSYCHOLOGY TODAY MAGAZINE. Copyright © 1976 American Psychological Association.

It was easy to believe in 1945 that Adolf Hitler's henchmen were mad. It seemed impossible, for example, that Albert Speer, Hitler's confidante, Reich Minister for Armaments and War Production, and the man personally responsible for enslaving millions could have been anything but a maniac. The lesson Hitler and the Nazis taught us seemed simple: keep insane people out of high office and the atrocities of the Third Reich will never happen again. Unfortunately, it wasn't that simple. The Nazis who went on trial at Nuremberg were as diverse a group of people as one might find in our own government today, or for that matter, in the leadership of the PTA.

In 1945, the Nazi war criminals took the Rorschach ink-blot test while they awaited trial. The Rorschach is a series of 10 cards with ink blots, some black and white, some with blobs of red, blue or yellow. The person being tested looks at each card and describes what the ink blot looks like to him. The ink blots are not intended to look like anything, so there is no right or wrong answer as there is, say, in an IQ test. The idea behind the Rorschach technique is that when a person describes what he sees, he reveals aspects of his personality, particularly his unconscious needs and desires.

Scorpions and Puppies

In 1947, 10 Rorschach experts, including myself, received copies of the Nazi Rorschach answers and were asked to comment on them. Although all of us agreed to respond, not one of us followed through. I was vice chairman of the committee that initiated this project, so my own failure to participate was particularly puzzling to me. Over the years, I have come to believe that our reason for not commenting on the test results was that they did not show what we expected to see, and what the pressure of public opinion demanded that we see — that these men were demented creatures, as different from normal people as a scorpion is different from a puppy. What we saw was a wide range of personalities, from severely disturbed neurotics to the superbly well-adjusted. But only Douglas Kelley, the Nuremberg psychiatrist who interviewed the Nazis, said aloud in 1946 "that such personalities are not unique or insane [and] could be duplicated in any country of the world today."

Over the past 30 years, psychologists have provided formidable evidence for the view that in the right circumstances ordinary people can commit acts far out of character. In the 1950s, social-psychologist Solomon Asch showed how readily most people will go along with a decision their own senses tell them is wrong. He asked college students to match the length of a line with one of three unequal lines. When working alone, people performed the feat with near-perfect accuracy. But when others, confederates of the experimenter, gave false answers, the accuracy level fell sharply. Only about a fourth of the students were unaffected by the majority judgments. Even when the majority was grossly in error, many people went along with the crowd. The Asch studies demonstrated that normal individuals will go along with a group decision even when that decision contradicts the testimony of their own eyes. And no coercion, no overt pressure, was needed to persuade people to share the majority view.

Authority Prevailed

Dr. [Stanley] Milgram never imagined that it would be so hard to get people to defy [his] commands. As he explained, "With numbing regularity good people were seen to knuckle under the demands of authority and perform actions that were callous and severe. Men who in everyday life are responsible and decent were seduced by the trappings of authority."

Jeanne Reinert, *Science Digest*, May 1970.

Guessing the length of a line is not the same as sending people to gas chambers, but recent studies by psychologist Stanley Milgram of the City University of New York come closer to showing how readily people can be induced to commit acts against an innocent individual. Milgram asked his volunteers to act as teachers while another person, actually a confederate of the experimenter, acted as the student. The volunteer was told that the object of the study was to determine the effects of punishment on learning. Each time the student, who was in another room, made an error, the teacher was to throw a switch giving the student an electric shock. With each error, the intensity of the shock increased. Of course, the confederate student did not actually get the shocks, but the teacher was made to believe that the shocks were real, painful and potentially lethal. As the shocks increased in intensity, the student would cry out in pain, pound on the wall and beg that the experiment end. But if the teacher hesitated to give a shock, the experimenter would urge him to continue. Sadly, most people did. In one experiment, 65 percent of Milgram's volunteers threw the highest switches, despite the written warning, "Danger: Severe Shock."

The notion that most people would never have committed the crimes of the Third Reich began to seem doubtful, and I wondered if there was any truth to the assumption that the Nazi horrors were the products of deranged minds.

In *The Nuremberg Mind*, psychologist Florence Miale and political-scientist Michael Selzer argue that the Nuremberg criminals were not only mentally disturbed, but that they shared a common personality. Their conclusions are based on their study of the Rorschach-test results.

War Criminals

In the hands of a skilled clinician, the Rorschach can be a sensitive diagnostic tool. But one problem with the Rorschach is that even a well-trained clinician can be influenced by what he expects to find. If he looks for evidence of sadism in the answers of a psychopathic murderer, the chances are that he will find it. To avoid this bias, Rorschach results must be scored "blind" — that is, without the Rorschach interpreter knowing who he is evaluating. Miale and Selzer did not use blind evaluation, and I suspected that their interpretations of the Rorschach results reflected their own expectations about Nazi mentality more than the personalities of the war criminals.

To find out, I sent the Rorschach records of eight war criminals along with eight other Rorschach records, to 15 acknowledged authorities in Rorschach interpretation. Ten of them agreed to participate. The Nazi records were the same ones used by Miale and Selzer in their book; the other records were those of people ranging in mental health from seriously disturbed to exceptionally well adjusted. Of course, my Rorschach experts were given no hint as to the backgrounds of the people tested, or that any of them might be war criminals, selecting those who seemed to be the most infamous: Rudolf Hess, Hitler's Deputy Fuehrer; Hermann Goering, Commander-in-Chief of the German air force and head of Hitler's Four-Year Plan to make Germany totally self-sufficient; Baldur von Schirach, Youth Leader of the Third Reich and later responsible for deporting Viennese Jews to extermination camps; Hjalmar Schacht, Minister of Economics, who was active in restricting the role of German Jews in business; Adolf Eichmann, SS Obersturmbannfuehrer, who was responsible for implementing the final solution; Albert Speer, Reich Minister for Armaments and War Production, Chief of the Nazi Party Technical Office and Hitler's personal architect; Joachim von Ribbentrop, Foreign Minister for Germany and an enthusiastic anti-Semite; and Constantin von Neurath, Protector for Bohemia and Moravia, responsible for keeping the Czech people under control.

139

Rating the Nazis

I arranged the 16 test records in two ways. One grouping was based on the degree of disturbance I found in the test records. Over the past three decades I have developed a system for evaluating Rorschach responses. The method has been validated on about 5,000 Rorschach records, including the test results of ministers, physicians, graduate psychology students, nurses, businessmen and other well-adjusted people, criminals in Sing Sing, juvenile delinquents, and 1,600 patients referred to me for testing.

I used this scale to evaluate the records of both war criminals and controls. I ranked the records from most well-adjusted to most severely disturbed and arranged them in groups of four. There were two Nazis in each group.

1. Superior personalities: Hjalmar Schacht, Minister of Economics; Clergyman and civil-rights leader; Baldur von Schirach, Youth Leader; Psychiatric patient, improved.

2. Normal personalities: Adolf Eichmann, SS Obersturmbannfuehrer; Clergyman and civil-rights leaders; Hermann Goering, Commander-in-Chief of German air force; Psychiatric patient, improved.

3. Less-than-adequate personalities: Rudolf Hess, Hitler's Deputy Fuehrer; Clergyman; Constantin von Neurath, Protector for Bohemia and Moravia; Hospitalized psychiatric patient.

4. Disturbed or impoverished personalities: Joachim von Ribbentrop, Foreign Minister; Clergyman; Albert Speer, Chief of Nazi Party Technical Office; Hospitalized psychiatric patient.

I asked the experts if they saw any similarity in these groupings and offered a checklist of 10 possible similarities, including war criminals, middle-class Americans, and superior adults in spotlight positions. Nine of the 10 judges said that the superior records were similar: six thought the similarity was that they were superior adults; two thought they were civil-rights leaders; one thought they were psychologists.

The experts described this group with comments such as "most sensitive and brightest," "adequate or better productiveness, fantasy, emotional responsiveness." Most experts also saw similarities in the other three groups (the normal, less than adequate, and most-disturbed personalities) that coincided with my rating system. Nine out of 10 believed that the sickest group showed some similarity. Comments included "extremely disturbed," "the most disturbed group," and "uniformly pathological."

The second grouping of test records reflected the backgrounds of the test takers: two groups of Nazis, four in each; a group of four clergymen; a group of four test records from two patients, one when each was disturbed, one when each was improved. I asked the experts to look at the test results in these four groups and note any similarity they saw within each. For the most part, the experts did not feel that the groupings reflected any commonality. Three experts saw a similarity in the first group of Nazis. However, one thought they were a cross section of middle-class Americans; another thought they were well-known superior adults; the third thought they were military men, but specified that they were not war criminals. One of the experts saw some similarity in the records of the second group of Nazis, but thought they could be members of the clergy.

Dangerous Belief

The results of this study show that the experts *were* able to detect mental disturbance from the Rorschach responses. If the Nazis shared a common, deranged mind, surely these experts would have seen some similarity in the two groups of Nazis. The fact that they didn't makes the notion that the war crimes were due to mental disorder untenable.

It is true that two of the Nazis, Joachim von Ribbentrop and Albert Speer, were rated as impoverished personalities by my own scoring system and by nine of the 10 judges. And it is possible that for these two men, their crimes expressed their neuroses. It is also possible that their symptoms were a reaction to the stress of awaiting trial. In any case, the other six Nazis showed no serious mental disturbance, and two of them were exceptionally well-adjusted. Their crimes cannot be blamed on mental disorder.

Hess, who was immature, oversensitive and suspicious, was not so different from many normally functioning individuals. And Goering, the Gestapo chief and head of the Luftwaffe, comes through on the Rorschach as a dynamic, rather crude man of action.

Unlike Hess, he was an insensitive fellow who lacked the ability for subtle emotional experiences. But during World War II I saw these same characteristics in many of our own decorated combat pilots.

These results do not excuse the acts of the Nazis. Instead, they demonstrate that well-adjusted people may get caught up in a tangle of social forces that makes them goose-step their way toward such abominations as the calculated execution of six million Jews and the systematic elimination of the elderly and other unproductive people. It may be comforting to believe that the horrors of World War II were the work of a dozen or so insane men, but it is a dangerous belief, one that may give us a false sense of security.

It *can* happen here.

Distinguishing Primary from Secondary Sources

A critical thinker must always question his or her source of knowledge. One way to critically evaluate information is to be able to distinguish between *primary sources* (a "firsthand" or eyewitness account from personal letters, documents, or speeches, etc.) and *secondary sources* (a "secondhand" account usually based upon a "firsthand" account and possibly appearing in newspapers, encyclopedias, or other similar types of publications). A diary about the Civil War written by a Civil War veteran is an example of a primary source. A history of the Civil War written many years after the war and relying, in part, upon that diary for information is an example of a secondary source.

However, it must be noted that interpretation and/or point of view also play a role when dealing with primary and secondary sources. For example, the historian writing about the Civil War not only will quote from the veteran's diary but also will interpret it. It is certainly a possibility that his or her interpretation may be incorrect. Even the diary or primary source must be questioned as to interpretation and point of view. The veteran may have been a militarist who stressed the glory of warfare rather than the human suffering involved.

This activity is designed to test your skill in evaluating sources of information. Pretend that you are writing a research paper on the nature of war crimes. You decide to include an equal number of primary and secondary sources. Listed below are a number of sources which may be useful in your research. Carefully evaluate each of them. First, place a *P* next to those descriptions you feel would serve as primary sources. Second, rank the primary sources assigning the number (1) to the most objective and accurate primary source, number (2) to the next accurate and so on until the ranking is finished. Repeat the entire procedure, this time placing an *S* next to those descriptions you feel would serve as secondary sources and then ranking them.

If you are doing this activity as a member of a class or group, discuss and compare your evaluation with other members of the group. If you are reading this book alone, you may want to ask others if they agree with your evaluation. Either way, you will find the interaction very valuable.

_____ 1. An eyewitness account of the atomic bombing of   _____
Hiroshima.

_____ 2. An historian writing a history of WW II in 1984.   _____

_____ 3. Articles by a war correspondent who interviewed   _____
members of Charlie Company shortly after the
Mylai episode.

_____ 4. A feature story in *Time* magazine dealing with the   _____
Mylai episode.

_____ 5. A speech by President Harry S. Truman explaining   _____
why he decided to drop the atomic bomb on
Hiroshima.

_____ 6. A poem describing the horrors of war written by a   _____
combat marine.

_____ 7. A journalist reporting on a statement by the Joint   _____
Chiefs of Staff.

_____ 8. A biography of President Harry S. Truman.   _____

_____ 9. The Treaty of Peace signed by the United States   _____
and Japan ending WW II.

_____ 10. Viewpoint four in this chapter.   _____

_____ 11. Viewpoint five in this chapter.   _____

_____ 12. A documentary film on the Vietnam War.   _____

Bibliography

The following list of books deals with the subject matter of this chapter.

William J. Bosch	*Judgement on Nuremberg.* Chapel Hill: North Carolina University Press, 1970.
Richard A. Falk, Gabriel Kolko and Robert Jay Lifton, eds.	*Crimes of War.* New York: Random House, 1971.
Ellen Kennedy	*After the Holocaust: Nazi War Crimes and the Limits of Guilt.* London: Robertson and Company, 1981.
Peter Kursten	*Law, Soldiers and Combat.* Westport, CT: Greenwood Publishing, 1978.
Daniel Lang	*Casualties of War.* New York: McGray-Hill, 1969.
H. S. Levie	*When Battle Rages How Can Law Protect?* Ferry, NY: Oceana Publications, 1971.
Richard B. Lyttle	*Nazi Hunting.* New York: Franklin Watts, 1982.
Richard H. Minear	*The Tokyo War Crimes Trial.* Princeton: Princeton University Press, 1971.
Inge S. Neumann	*European War Crimes Trials: A Bibliography.* Westport, CT: Greenwood Publishing, 1978.
Adam Roberts and Richard Guelff, eds.	*Documents on the Laws of War.* New York: Oxford University Press. 1982.
Leighton Rollins	*Disasters of War.* Santa Barbara: Cadmus Editions, 1981.
Dorothy Schaffter	*War and Military Courts: Judicial Interpretation of Its Meaning.* Smithtown, NY: Exposition Press, 1980.
Peter D. Trooboff, ed.	*Law and Responsibility in Warfare: The Vietnam Experience.* Chapel Hill, NC: University of North Carolina Press, 1975.
Western Goals	*The War Called Peace; The Soviet Peace Offensive,* Alexandria, VA: Western Goals, 1982.

Are Peace Movements Effective?

"Our survival depends on worldwide concern and political mobilization forcing governments to view nuclear proliferation as irrational behavior."

Why Peace Movements Are Needed

Mark E. Thompson

Mark E. Thompson, who has a Ph.D. in education, has written numerous articles on education and several essays on nuclear weaponry. Some of his views are derived from the ten years he spent as a nuclear weapons officer in the US Air Force. Dr. Thompson is currently chief of employee development, Office of the Inspector General, US Department of Agriculture. In the following viewpoint, he explains why active participation by all peoples is necessary to lead the world out of the "lethel nuclear cul-de-sac" into which humanity has driven itself.

As you read, consider the following questions:

1. Why does the author believe that people "sense no danger from nuclear weapons?"
2. According to the author, what is humanity's Achilles heel?
3. Do you agree with the author? Why or why not?

Mark E. Thompson, "A Question of Survival". Reprinted from USA TODAY, September 1982. Copyright 1982 by Society for the Advancement of Education.

Since 1945 and the destruction of thousands of lives with atomic weapons, we have greatly increased our capability to destroy life with nuclear weapons. It has been reported that we have about 30,000 nuclear warheads and the Soviet Union probably has an equal number. England, and France, India, China, Israel, and perhaps South Africa collectively have many thousands of nuclear weapons. All this is enough destructive power to destroy our planet several times over. Aldous Huxley once said that man is unique in organizing the mass murder of his own species. . . .

Survival is now threatened by nuclear weapons, but there is relatively little concern or sense of emergency expressed by our country or by the world community. Our survival instincts seem to be important in a nuclear age that threatens us with a quick, unexpected technical death. Technology has anesthetized our instincts for survival with the elusion of technological hope. We are content to *hope* a nuclear war will not happen. Our primitive survival instincts and our highly developed intellectual powers have failed to protect us from a possible nuclear holocaust in the future.

Most people sense no danger from nuclear weapons, just as we do not suspect danger from our refrigerator or egg beater. Products of technology, as we are told and as we have come to understand, are developed for the good of mankind. They represent progress. Industrialists and military leaders all but proclaim heresy if technology is accused of producing flawed instruments of destruction. Their central argument in the case of nuclear weapons is that adequate controls exist to prevent a nuclear war (i.e., the existence of a hot line between Russia and the U.S. will solve problems; the risk of nuclear war in the world is so dangerous that no nation will start one; and, by being strong, no one will dare use nuclear weapons on us). . . .

Humanity's Achilles Heel

Nuclear weapons are more than extremely dangerous technical products. They represent the Achilles heel of humanity. Survival instincts in a technical environment must be extra-sensitive to the demanding nature of technology—e.g., technology can subtly exploit humans within a flawed universe. Technology forces change in our behavior patterns, but at times we are slow to react. Human control and concern are not keeping up with technical innovation.

In the case of nuclear weapons, the entire concept of warfare has changed, but few understand what has happened. The traditional doctrine of having military superiority is not possible with nuclear weapons when both sides have the capability to destroy each other several times over. This means that improvements in delivery systems, weapons design sophistication, and numerical superiority do not guarantee a definitive military advantage. If it only takes a handful of nuclear weapons to destroy a large country like Russia, why do we need nearly 30,000 such weapons? We think we need them because military strategists say our safety depends on the capability to destroy our enemy many times over—i.e., we must be sure that our weapons will survive their weapons. The Soviet Union thinks the same thing, so we have matched each other in a global arms race the likes of which has never been seen before. We are locked with Russia in a deadly nuclear arms race that seems sure to kill off both of us and perhaps most of the world. . . .

No Easy Task

The war against war is going to be no holiday excursion or camping party. The military feelings are too deeply grounded to abdicate their place among our ideals until better substitutes are offered than the glory and shame that come to nations as well as individuals from the ups and downs of politics and the vicissitudes of trade.

William James, *The Moral Equivalent of War.*

An understanding of this condition has alerted the survival instincts of some thoughtful people around the world (many in Europe), but there are also many citizens who do not believe they are threatened. The hidden satanic nature of this dormant technological problem is insidious. People have difficulty understanding the potential danger of any technical problem, because technology is consistently expressed as a positive good. Our survival instincts are not sensitive to the dangers of a nuclear war, because we do not understand or comprehend the possibility of such an event. People do not dwell on the subject of nuclear war, just as they do not think about their own death. The subject is remote, unpleasant, and not easy to understand. Japanese living in Hiroshima and Nagasaki have visual reminders of what nuclear weapons can do, and they are extremely sensitive. . . .

Politicians all over the world do not seem to comprehend the significance or urgency of this nuclear problem. A nuclear brontosaurus is now in our midst. Survival of our civilization depends on not having any kind of nuclear war (limited or unlimited). There may be no such thing as a limited nuclear war, just as we can not have a limited or confined technical world. Technology is not merely the means of power—it is power, and nuclear weapons are the zenith. . . .

Our survival and the survival of future generations will be assured only when nuclear weapons do not exist. Our Earth may not be able to recover from a nuclear war. William Barrett puts in this way: "Despite the great triumphs of a technical civilization, humankind still exists in the bosom of nature. We are creatures utterly dependent upon a delicate planetary environment—a thin crust of soil and a fragile layer of atmosphere."

The question of survival within the nuclear age brings a new conceptual problem to our attention. Since there are few observable or obvious signs that a serious problem exists, it is difficult to know about the problem. We will know about the problem when it is too late, as in the case of a nuclear war that would be over within 15 minutes. The sudden, execrable mishap at Three Mile Island is a good example, but not nearly so dangerous as nuclear war.

How is it possible to dismantle a weapons technology that thrives on paranoia and passionate intensity? It may not be possible at all. If conflict is endemic in the human race, as many believe, then more and more nuclear weapons will be built. Aggression—an old, but strong, survival instinct from our evolutionary past—does not serve us well when dealing with sophisticated technology. . . .

People Must Mobilize

Our survival within this extreme situation depends on worldwide concern and political mobilization forcing governments to view nuclear proliferation as a nefarious, irrational behavior. There will be little or no support of this approach from military-technical groups around the world. The struggle to eliminate nuclear weapons is countered by military-technical demands for more sophisticated weapons systems. The arguments are world safety vs. national security.

Our military believes that survival depends on having more nuclear weapons than Russia. The Russian military, from their perspective, holds the same convictions. Knowing for sure who has more weapons or better weapons and delivery systems is not possible; neither is it useful. Differences in strength between two nuclear superpowers are not meaningful. Each can kill the other many times over. Contrived differences are used by politicians as justification for further escalation. The Kennedy

Artists for Nuclear Disarmament

Daily World. May 19. 1982.

Administration did this when they got into office, and others now continue to use these scare tactics in the name of national defense. As William James said. "If a difference makes no difference, there is no difference."

Being able to reduce nuclear armaments through world opinion is perhaps the best way out of a terrible mess. Having faith that a nuclear war will not start by accident due to an impulsive military commander *a la* Dr. Strangelove fiction or some terrorist scheme is unreasonable. Scholars working in the history and philosophy of science have moved in the direction that no knowledge is ever certain and no proof is above suspicion. Nuclear war is not impossible, and it could start by accident.

The dilemma for concerned citizens is that general warnings, occasional demonstrations, and token gestures of arms reductions do not have much effect. This seems to confirm that we do not have just an extreme situation with nuclear weapons; we have a tragic situation.

Now, there is new meaning attached to the conceptual tragic sense of life. Nuclear weapons place an urgent added dimension to life's dark side. Everyone is a potential victim within the demonic nuclear crosshair and, as quick as it takes to flip a light switch, nuclear war can begin. A question of survival will be moot when the lights go out and the nuclear glow begins . . . .

"It was the peace movement that paved the way to war."

Peace Movements Can Lead to War

Ed Fredricks

Ed Fredricks experienced international politics first-hand as a vice-consul at the American Embassy in Seoul, South Korea and later as a political officer in the United Nations section of the Department of State. He is a state senator in Michigan. In the following viewpoint, Senator Fredricks points to events leading up to World War II to illustrate why peace movements can be perceived as a paralysis of will by a nations' adversaries.

As you read, consider the following questions:

1. According to William L. Shirer, what was Hitler's first objective regarding his adversaries?
2. What examples does Mr. Shirer offer to support his claims?
3. According to the author, what lessons can be learned from the World War II experience with Hitler?
4. Do you agree with the author? Why or why not?

Ed Fredricks, "Peace Movements Can Pave the Way to War", May 14, 1983. Reprinted with permission from *Human Events*.

Sen. Edward M. Kennedy told a nuclear freeze crowd on the Capitol lawn that President Reagan's arms reduction policy is "voodoo arms control" and concluded that "the case is overwhelmingly for a freeze now, and then for reductions that are so essential."

His brother and late President John F. Kennedy wrote a book in 1940 entitled *Why England Slept,* which chronicled Great Britain's alarming failure to see the coming of World War II. Sen. Kennedy should read this book.

While Sen. Kennedy leads the assault against nuclear weapons, there are, of course, no demonstrations against nuclear war in the Soviet Union. This gives totalitarian regimes an edge, which John Kennedy identified as the primary shortcoming of free nations.

"In the first place," he began, "democracy is essentially peace loving; the people don't want to go to war. . . . The hatred of war is, in this day of modern warfare, a great disadvantage. . . . The result is that people, because of their hatred of war, will not permit armaments to be built. They are so determined to stay out that they cannot look ahead to the day when they will find occasion to fight."

The father of John and Ted Kennedy, Joseph P. Kennedy, had served as United States Ambassador to Great Britain from 1938 to 1940, when Ted Kennedy was from six to eight years old. The senator and his family saw England first-hand nearly engulfed by a war which it should have foreseen but for which it was not prepared. John Kennedy was undoubtedly helped by access to the inner sanctums of the policy-makers, and in fact in August 1939 returned from a visit to Berlin to tell his father that war would break out within a week, which it did.

"We must be prepared to recognize democracy's weaknesses in competition with a totalitarian form of government," continued Kennedy in his book. "We must realize that one is a system geared for peace, the other for war. . . .It means that in preparing for war today, a democracy may be struck such a knockout blow by a totalitarian form of government. Especially it is complicated by the fact that a democracy's free press gives the speeches of the totalitarian leaders, who state their case in such a 'reasonable' manner that it is hard always to see them as a menace."

An Example to Remember

When Hitler moved into the Rhineland on March 7, 1936, he proved that well. Already in May 1933 he had given his first "peace" speech, in response to a peace appeal by American President Franklin Roosevelt.

William L. Shirer, in *The Rise and Fall of the Third Reich,* states that Hitler's first objective "was to confound Germany's adversaries in Europe by preaching disarmament and peace." He warmly thanked Roosevelt for his peace initiative, and asserted "Germany would be perfectly ready to disband her entire military establishment and destroy the small amount of arms remaining to her, if the neighboring countries will do the same... because she does not think of attacking but only of acquiring security."

"The world was enchanted," Shirer recounts, "and amongst the London papers *The Times, Daily Herald* and weekly *Spectator* there was "rejoicing."

On May 21, 1935, in another "peace" speech Hitler eloquently insisted that "Germany needs peace and desires peace!" These words were "lapped up" in the western democracies of Europe, according to Shirer, while the *Times* of London "welcomed them with almost hysterical joy."

So the climate was set. The West was panting for peace, and not prepared to keep it. Early on March 7, 1936, Hitler's troops marched into the Rhineland. At 10:00 a.m. German Foreign Minister Konstantin von Neurath apprised the ambassadors of France, Britain and Italy of the German action. "Two hours later," continued Shirer, "the Fuehrer was standing at the rostrum of the Reichstag before a delirious audience expounding on his desire for peace and his latest ideas of how to maintain it."

Had the free world not been so mesmerized by Hitler's cries for peace, World War II would have been stopped cold, and tens of millions of lives saved.

"The 48 hours after the march into the Rhineland" someone heard Hitler say, "were the most nerve-racking in my life. If the French had then marched into the Rhineland, we would have had to withdraw with our tails between our legs, for the military resources at our disposal would have been wholly inadequate for even a moderate resistance."

Shirer wrote: "In March 1936 the two western democracies were given their last chance to halt, without the risk of a serious war, the rise of a militarized, aggressive, totalitarian Germany and in fact — as we have seen Hitler admitting — bring the Nazi dictator and his regime tumbling down. They let the chance slip by."

Former British Prime Minister Winston Churchill states that the British were told then by the French that "according to French information, the German troops in the Rhineland had orders to withdraw if opposed in a forcible manner." But Churchill recalled that British Prime Minister Stanley Baldwin explained to the French that "he was able to interpret accurately the feelings of the British people. And they want peace."

A False Notion

If we apply to the prewar period the theory expressed by today's so-called "peace" movement we would be forced to conclude that the greatest threat to peace between 1935 and 1939 was not Adolf Hitler but Winston Churchill. The falsity of this idea should now be apparent to all, as should be the falsity of its modern descendant, that the United States is the principal threat to peace today. If the United States were a threat to peace, the hegemony of the Soviet Union would not have survived that period between 1945 and 1960 when the United States possessed a virtual monopoly on nuclear weapons and sufficient power to bring the Kremlin to heel at any time it so desired.

The prehistory of the Second World War is extremely instructive about the objective consequences of peace movements: the horrors of the First World War were followed by a vigorous and superficially successful peace movement. . . . The advocates of "peace" so prevailed in the democracies that at every turn, Hitler's demands were satisfied without firing a shot. And just twenty-one years after the guns fell silent, Europe was at war again.

John R. Silber, "Apocalypses Then and Now," *Public Opinion*, August/September 1982.

Churchill also observed that "The *Times* and *Daily Herald*. . . expressed their belief in the sincerity of Hitler's offers of a non-aggressive pact," and that future Prime Minister Naville Chamberlain emphasized to the French foreign minister that British "public opinion would not support us in sanctions of any kind." So it was the *peace* movement that paved the way to war!

No Real Difference

But it is not different now? Are not the peace demonstrations today because of the total destructiveness of nuclear war? Well, according to John Kennedy's book, in the 1930s it was the bomber that absolutely terrified the people. Baldwin emphasized in a speech that "There is no power on earth which can protect [one] from being bombed . . . the bomber will always get through

. . . . The only defense is in offense, which means that you have to kill more women and children more quickly than the enemy if you want to save yourselves." "The sense of hopelessness in this thought," said Kennedy, "profoundly impressed the people. It struck them with a feeling of horror towards a war and especially was this directed against the air arm."

But Kennedy reveals in his book that Baldwin later admitted he was "worried" by the Hitler buildup. Why didn't he do something? He quotes Baldwin: "I cannot think of anything that would have made the loss of the election [!] from my point of view more certain." If Baldwin was "worried," Kennedy says it was his duty to go to the public in the 1935 election on that issue alone, or "it puts him in the role of deceiving the public and playing politics with the country's welfare."

That's a strong message that Kennedy gives to all of us. When the book was first printed in 1940, Henry Luce wrote in the foreward he hoped one million Americans would read the book. Well, if one American, his brother, would read it, John F. Kennedy will have done this nation a great service.

At the same rally at which Sen. Kennedy spoke, Congressman Robert Torricelli of New Jersey pleaded: "I want Ronald Reagan to hear a *desperate* voice of the American people. . . ." Indeed, it may be desperate. Shirer used that very word to describe how in pre-war Europe the "people and their governments *desperately* yearned for the continuance of peace." but President Kennedy underlined as our "weakness" our propensity to become desperate.

The evidence is clear. Mao Tse-tung once said about nuclear war: "Perhaps even more than half [of humanity] will perish . . . but imperialism would be destroyed entirely. . . . China would be the last nation to die."

The Soviets have prepared an elaborate underground civil defense network while we have barely given it thought. Leonid Brezhnev predicted that "by 1985, as a consequence of what we are now achieving with detente. . .we will be able to exert our will wherever we need to."

A Time for Strength

The Berlin Wall still stands and people who leave East Germany are shot; Eastern Europe is a prison. And now the evidence becomes clearer that the attempt on the life of Pope John Paul II may have come from the Soviet KGB, then headed by Yuri Andropov, who is now in charge of the Soviet Union.

At the same time, people flock to the United States. Yet

freedom is in retreat, and stands maligned at the United Nations and around the world. Apparently the people of the world and their leaders have different agendas. Freedom as known in the United States is obviously the agenda of the people of the world.

It is our challenge with our free speech and free press to confront the weakness of our freedoms as defined by Kennedy and convert them into the obvious strength that they can be and should be.

"Our objectives must be to free Europe from confrontation, to enforce detente between the United States and the Soviet Union, and, ultimately, to dissolve both great power alliances."

Peace Movements Are Necessary for Survival

European Nuclear Disarmament Committee

Deployment of American nuclear missiles on the border of Western Europe evokes increasingly heated discussion and demonstrations. On the one hand, proponents of the deployment argue that the missiles will make Europeans more secure since the missiles would deter a conventional attack. On the other hand, anti-nuclear missiles will encourage a buildup of missiles on the Russian side of the border, thus making a European nuclear war *more* likely. The following viewpoint appeals for nuclear disarmament in Europe and explains why disarmament is necessary.

As you read, consider the following questions:

1. Who does the author blame for the current arms race?
2. According to the author, what steps must the superpowers take to diminish the likelihood of war?
3. Who, according to the author, must be responsible for a nuclear-free Europe?

This viewpoint is the text of an appeal for European Nuclear Disarmament launched on April 28, 1980.

We are entering the most dangerous decade in human history. A third world war is merely possible, but increasingly likely. Economic and social difficulties in advanced industrial countries, crisis, militarism, and war in the third world compound the political tensions that fuel a demented arms race. In Europe, the main geographical state for the East-West confrontation, new generations of even more deadly nuclear weapons are appearing.

For at least twenty-five years, the forces of both the North Atlantic and the Warsaw alliance have each had sufficient nuclear weapons to annihilate their opponents, and at the same time to endanger the very basis of civilized life. But with each passing year, competition in nuclear armaments has multiplied their numbers, increasing the probability of some devastating accident or miscalculation.

As each side tries to prove its readiness to use nuclear weapons, in order to prevent their use by the other side, new, more "usable" nuclear weapons are designed and the idea of "limited" nuclear war is made to sound more and more plausible. So much so that this paradoxical process can logically only lead to the actual use of nuclear weapons.

Neither of the major powers is now in any moral position to influence smaller countries to forgo the acquisition of nuclear armament. The increasing spread of nuclear reactors and the growth of the industry that installs them, reinforce the likelihood of world wide proliferation of nuclear weapons, thereby multiplying the risks of nuclear exchanges.

Over the years, public opinion has pressed for nuclear disarmament and detente between the contending military blocs. This pressure has failed. An increasing proportion of world resources is expended on weapons, even though mutual extermination is already amply guaranteed. This economic burden, in both East and West, contributes to growing social and political strain, setting in motion a vicious circle in which the arms race feeds upon the instability of the world economy and vice versa: a deathly dialectic.

Too Great a Danger

We are now in great danger. Generations have been born beneath the shadow of nuclear war, and have become habituated to the threat. Concern has given way to apathy. Meanwhile, in a world living always under menace, fear extends through both halves of the European continent. The powers of the military and of internal security forces are enlarged, limitations are placed upon free exchanges of ideas and between persons, and civil rights of independent-minded individuals are threatened, in the West as well as the East.

We do not wish to apportion guilt between the political and military leaders of East and West. Guilt lies squarely upon both parties. Both parties have adopted menacing postures and committed aggressive actions in different parts of the world.

The remedy lies in our own hands. We must act together to free the entire territory of Europe, from Poland to Portugal, from nuclear weapons, air and submarine bases, and from all institutions engaged in research into or manufacture of nuclear weapons. We ask the two superpowers to withdraw all nuclear weapons from European territory. In particular, we ask the Soviet Union to halt production of SS-20 medium-range missiles and we ask the United States not to implement the decision to develop cruise missiles and Pershing II missiles for deployment in Western Europe. We also urge the ratification of the SALT II agreement, as a necessary step toward the renewal of effective negotiations on general and complete disarmament.

At the same time, we must defend and extend the right of all citizens, East or West, to take part in this common movement and to engage in every kind of exchange.

We appeal to our friends in Europe, of every faith and persuasion, to consider urgently the ways in which we can work together for these common objectives. We envisage a European-wide campaign, in which every kind of exchange takes place; in which representatives of different nations and opinions confer and coordinate their activities; and in which less formal exchanges, between universities, churches, women's organizations, trade unions, youth organizations, professional groups, and individuals, take place with the object of promoting a common object: to free all of Europe from nuclear weapons.

We must commence to act as if a united, neutral, and pacific Europe already exits. We must learn to be loyal, not to "East" or "West," but to each other, and we must disregard the prohibitions and limitations imposed by any national state.

A Responsibility for All

It will be the responsiblility of the people of each nation to agitate for the expulsion of nuclear weapons and bases from European soil and territorial waters, and to decide upon its own means and strategy, concerning its own territory. These will differ from one country to another, and we do not suggest that any single strategy should be imposed. But this must be part of a

Ollie Harrington, *Daily World*.

transcontinental movement in which every kind of exchange takes place.

We must resist any attempt by the statesmen of East or West to manipulate this movement to their own advantage. We offer no advantage to either NATO or the Warsaw alliance. Our objectives must be to free Europe from confrontation, to enforce detente between the United States and the Soviet Union, and, ultimately, to dissolve both great power alliances.

In appealing to fellow-Europeans, we are not turning our

backs on the world. In working for the peace of Europe we are working for peace of the world. Twice in this century Europe has disgraced its claims to civilization by engendering world war. This time we must repay our debts to the world by engendering peace.

This appeal will achieve nothing if it is not supported by determined and inventive action, to win more people to support it. We need to mount an irresistible pressure for a Europe free of nuclear weapons.

We do not wish to impose any uniformity on the movement nor to preempt the consultations and decisions of those many organizations already exercising their influence for disarmament and peace. But the situation is urgent. The dangers steadily advance. We invite your support for this common objective, and we shall welcome both your help and advice.

"A study of the history of peace movements challenges one's ability to be optimistic."

Why Peace Movements Fail

James Clotfelter

James Clotfelter draws from his broad background in political science to present his perspective on peace movements. His Ph.D. is from the University of North Carolina at Chapel Hill and he is currently a professor of political science at the University of North Carolina at Greensboro. Dr. Clotfelter is the author of several books and articles including *The Military in American Politics*. In the following viewpoint, he takes a pessimistic view of the influences peace movements have exerted on world events.

As you read, consider the following questions:

1. According to the author, what three unavoidable problems face all national peace movements?
2. According to the author, what seven avoidable problems face peace movements?
3. What two reasons does the author himself offer to explain the failure of peace movements?

Peace movements thrive, an English writer has observed, when there is both optimism and pessimism: optimism, because there must be hope that shooting can be averted, that steps can be taken toward a more peaceful world; pessimism, because there must be clouds of war to spur interest in peace issues, to move us out of our normal preoccupation with more pleasant topics.

If this analysis is correct, then Europe's peace demonstrations might mark the renewal of a strong peace movement on that continent. And we might see a reinvigorated peace movement in the United States. Americans are chronic optimists; that requirement is easily met. Pessimism comes harder for us, but the Reagan arms buildup, events in Poland and Central America, and press attention to nuclear war have made the dangers more obvious.

Assume that frightening federal deficits force reductions in the rate of increase in Pentagon spending for the next fiscal year. What then? What will become of this prospering American peace movement?

If it follows the pattern of past peace movements, this one will affect some policies and will move some people, but it will ultimately fail to avert war or to build a broad peace.

Peace movements of the 20th century generally have been unable to achieve their immediate objectives, and have had even less impact on long-term public policy. Wars ultimately end, but rarely because of the work of peace movements. These movements in the United States and Europe have failed because they lack numbers, influence and access to power, or because they lack the programs to hold both popular and elite support. Why is this so?

Why Peace Movements Fail

Some problems facing national peace movements, I would argue, are unavoidable and thus not worth much attention. One is their inability to reconcile the fact that they are asking a *nation* for action with the fact that the action has *international* dimensions. There is no way around this problem, but it confronts proponents of military solutions as well. A second inevitable weakness of peace movements is their factionalism. I see no cure for this ill; it must be endured where it is troublesome, and exploited where it is helpful. Third, it is claimed that the peace movement is all heart and no head, that it is weak on realistic analysis. Peace activists should avoid the purely sentimental and the wildly hyperbolic. Regardless of their efforts at rigor, however, peace activists will ultimately call on people to make decisions with their hearts as well as their heads.

A look at seven possibly avoidable causes for the failure of peace movements might suggest new approaches for the future. The first two are the extremes of the continuum of consonance with national values. The third is the time perspective. The last four relate to appeals and symbols used by or forced on the movement.

1. *Peace movements fail because they are not seen as reflecting the basic values of a society.* This was the case with the pre-1914 movement in Germany, widely identified as foreign in its spirit and impetus. This hazard can never be entirely eliminated, because peacemaking is foreign to some values of all nations. There are indigenous peace themes in the history of the English-speaking countries that did not exist in Germany, but the American and English themes are those of a tolerated minority rather than of the dominant culture.

2. *Peace movements fail because they identify with such widely approved national symbols and themes as to deny themselves a clear identity.* This situation describes the pre-1914 peace movement in the United States. Presidents Taft and Wilson and five secretaries of state between 1905 and 1914 were members of peace societies. Yet in 1917, when the United States entered the European war, only a small number of socialists, social reformers and religious pacifists maintained that a peace movement must of necessity oppose war.

3. *Peace movements fail because they focus on the past, the present or the distant future, rather than the intermediate future.* Each time perspective has its own hazards. But I am asserting, without benefit here of evidence, that the focus should be on the intermediate future: later than next year, sooner than the withering away of the state. . . .

4. *Peace movements fail because they are unable, or unwilling, to convince people that wars hurt economies.* "Business pacifism" was part of pre-1914 peace sentiment in the United States and western Europe. Norman Angell, in the *The Great Illusion*, argued that wars destroy prosperity, even for the victor. As the president of the National Association of Manufacturers (U.S.) commented, "Dead men buy no clothes." After World War II, which stimulated the American economy and created jobs, "business pacifism" was almost obliterated in America, and President Eisenhower's identification of a "military-industrial complex" seemed to confirm that war is good for business. Yet the Vietnam war severely damaged the American economy, and by

1968 radical proposals on Vietnam were appearing in *Forbes* and the *Wall Street Journal.* Peace activists of the 1960s were slow to argue that war, although it benefits some, has a negative net effect on the economy. Perhaps they were reluctant to appeal to people's self-interest, or perhaps they were slow to believe that economic self-interest could work against war.

5. *Peace movements fail because they fail to bridge class and ideological divisions.* The class and ideological characteristics of peace activists are well known. Activists usually are from the middle class; in the United States they tend to be white, from the northeast or from large cities in the west and midwest; women college students and "modernist" Protestant clergy have been conspicuously represented. In political ideology (except for pre-1914 America), peace movements have drawn disproportionately from the radical left. None of these characteristics is inevitably associated with peacemaking. All are cause and effect of the minority status of peace movements.

6. *Peace movements fail because they become identified with threatening symbols unrelated to peace.* By 1967 the antiwar movement in America had become stereotyped as a band of long-haired, profane, pot-smoking kids in revolt against the older

Ben Sargent, *Austin American Statesman.* Reprinted with permission.

generation and its institutions. Whereas participants in the civil rights movement a few years earlier had combed their hair and curbed their tongues to present a positive public image, the antiwar activists sought to shock and in some cases to offend. The result was that while the Vietnam war was unpopular, the antiwar movement was even less popular—and the style of some activists may have deterred working-class and rural Americans from moving to an antiwar stance.

7. *Peace movements fail because they become identified with appeasement of national adversaries.* This charge often is made unjustly, but it remains a difficult one for peace activists to deal with. The pre-1914 German peace movement, when it was noticed at all, was attacked as a stooge for the English. The appeasement charge was particularly unjust at the time of World War II, for American peace activists had been outspoken critics of Hitler and of the Munich agreement. But if it was unjust to link peace work and appeasement in the '40s, the suspicion was more understandable in the '60s, when some American antiwar activists made no effort to conceal their sympathies for an authoritarian regime in North Vietnam.

So much for what may be empirically verifiable. Other flaws in peace movements can be evaluated only subjectively. I am identifying two that frequently concern peace advocates. To the extent that these flaws exist, they are, I suggest, the most serious ones; however, they are now widely recognized. My first assertion below is conventional wisdom in some circles, and the second reflects one of the oldest articles of Christian faith.

1. *Peace movements fail because they work for a "peace" too narrowly defined.* Too often in the past, peace has been defined as order—as the absence of conflict, even as the absence of change. Given the inevitability and in some instances the desirability of conflict and change, this concept of peace fails on both empirical and normative grounds The pre-1914 French, German and American peace movements all possessed an unduly legalistic notion of what peace involved. The same could be said of the more respectable elements of the post-1945 movement in the U.S. A better concept would be some variation of "peace with justice" (amply discussed in available literature).

2. *Peace movements fail because they dwell on fear rather than hope.* Just as peace movements need both optimism and pessimism to thrive, it is inevitable that in their appeals fear will be mixed with hope. But introducing fear in popular appeals is like introducing poison gas to a battlefield on a gusty day. Fear produces unstable and unpredictable results. In America in

1938-1941, for example, fear of war generated support for such disparate goals as peace, isolation and military involvement.

The recent discovery of nuclear war by television and mass-circulation magazines, and efforts to publicize the consequences of nuclear war through Ground Zero and university teach-ins, have brought war concerns to a wider audience. The risk is that this attention will encourage fear without giving grounds for hope, that it will stimulate anxiety without providing a constructive release for that anxiety.

The fact that peace movements persist despite their failures is a tribute to the capacity of peace activists to sustain hope. Nonetheless, a study of the history of peace movements challenges one's ability to be optimistic.

Recognizing Stereotypes

A stereotype is an oversimplified or exaggerated description of people or things. Stereotyping can be favorable. However, most stereotyping tends to be highly uncomplimentary and, at times, degrading.

Stereotyping grows out of our prejudices. When we stereotype someone, we are prejudging him or her. Consider the following example: Mr. X is convinced that all Mexicans are lazy, sloppy and careless people. The Diaz family, a family of Mexicans, happen to be his next-door neighbors. One evening, upon returning home from work, Mr. X notices that the garbage pails in the Diaz driveway are overturned and that the rubbish is scattered throughout the driveway. He immediately says to himself: "Isn't that just like those lazy, sloppy and careless Mexicans?" The possibility that a group of neighborhood vandals or a pack of stray dogs may be responsible for the mess never enters his mind. Why not? Simply because he has prejudged all Mexicans and will keep his stereotype consistent with his prejudice. The famous (or infamous) Archie Bunker of television fame is a classic example of our Mr. X.

The following statements relate to the subject matter in this chapter. Consider each statement carefully. *Mark S for any statement that is an example of stereotyping. Mark N for any statement that is not an example of stereotyping. Mark U if you are undecided about any statement.*

If you are doing this activity as a member of a class or group, compare your answers with those of other class or group members. Be able to defend your answers. You may discover that others will come to different conclusions than you. Listening to the reasons others present for their answers may give you valuable insights in recognizing stereotypes.

If you are reading this book alone, ask others if they agree with your answers. You too will find this interaction very valuable.

S = *stereotype*
N = *not a stereotype*
U = *undecided*

1. Nations which possess nuclear weapons are merely interested in defending themselves.

2. Modern technology is a curse to humanity because it has been responsible for the development of nuclear weapons.

3. If politicians were more like "ordinary" citizens, they would dismantle all nuclear weapons.

4. Virtually all sane, rational people would do all in their power to avoid a nuclear war.

5. Soviet leaders do not really care if there is a third world war involving nuclear weapons.

6. American leaders are usually on the side of truth and justice in their decisions on issues of war and peace.

7. People involved in peace movements are, on the whole, gentle and caring in their actions toward others.

8. Most nations will act in their own self interest.

9. Russia has always been a callous outlaw among nations.

10. An all-out nuclear war will most likely benefit no person or nation.

11. Peace movements fail because they do not reflect the basic values of a society.

12. If decisions on war and peace were left to women alone, there probably would never be war.

13. One of the primary reasons that humanity has been involved in so many wars is that the overwhelming majority of world leaders have been men.

14. If there is ever a nuclear war, it probably will have an accidental cause.

Bibliography

The following list of books deals with the subject matter of this chapter.

Cronbach, Abraham — *The Quest for Peace*, Englewood, NJ: Jerome S. Ozer, Publisher Inc., 1972.

Elazar, Daniel J. — *Cam David Framework for Peace: A Shift Toward Shared Rule*, Washington, DC: American Enterprise Institute for Public Policy Research, 1979.

Erasmus, Desiderius — *The Complaint of Peace*, Norwood, NJ: Walter J. Johnson Inc., 1973.

Guinan, Edward, ed. — *Peace & Non-Vilence: Basic Writings*, Ramsey, NJ: Paulist Press, 1973.

Hedemann, Ed, ed. — *Guide to War Tax Resistance*, New York: War Resistors, 1982.

Kashieu, Yu — *After Fourteen Thousand Wars*, (Progress Publications, USSR) Chicago: Imported Publications, 1979.

Manning, C. A. — *Peaceful Change*, New York: Garland Publishing, Inc., 1973.

May, Mark — *A Social Psychology of War and Peace*, New York: Garland Publishing, Inc., 1972.

Merritt, Richard L. and Russett, Bruce M., eds. — *From National Development to Global Community*, Winchester, MA: Allen Unwin, Inc., 1981.

Milne, A. A. — *Peace with Honour*, New York: Garland Publishing, Inc., 1972.

Peachey, J. Lorne — *How to Teach Peace to Children*, Scottdale, PA: Herald Press, 1981.

Waskow, Arthur — *The Worried Man's Guide to World Peace*, Magnolia, MA: Peter Smith, Publisher, Inc.

UNESCO — *UNESCO Yearbook on Peace and Conflict Studies*, Westport, CT: Greenwood Press, 1980.

Can War Be Eliminated?

"The most feasible approach to drastically reducing the possibility of war is to limit armaments to those useful only for defense."

A Defensive Weapons System Can Eliminate War

Harry B. Hollins

Harry B. Hollins has long been involved in world politics, most recently as a member of the executive committee of the Institute for World Order in New York. In the following viewpoint, Mr. Hollins claims that armaments should be reduced to a bare minimum, so that they can be used only for defense.

As you read, consider the following questions:

1. What is the McCloy-Zorin proposal?
2. What is the principle feature of the defensive weapons system?
3. Why does the author believe that the defensive weapons system might be acceptable to the world's governments?
4. Do you believe that the defensive weapons system can insure peace? Why or why not?

"A Defensive Weapons Systems" by Harry B. Hollins, June/July, 1982. Reprinted by permission of THE BULLETIN OF THE ATOMIC SCIENTISTS, a magazine of science and public affairs. Copyright © 1982 by the Educational Foundation for Nuclear Science, Chicago, Ill., 60637.

The most notable arms control treaties since World War II are: the Partial Test Ban Treaty, 1963; the Treaty on the Non-Proliferation of Nuclear Weapons, 1968; and the Anti-Ballistic Missile Treaty and the Interim Agreement on the Limitation of Strategic Offensive Missiles (both SALT I), 1972. The purpose of these treaties is to modify the international security system to make it less dangerous, not to change the competitive armaments system with its high reliance on devastating the enemy. Despite these treaties, the last 25 years have witnessed the development of increasingly destructive weapons systems, the accumulation of huge nuclear arsenals by the great powers, and military expenditures at $500 billion annually. Not a single weapon has been destroyed as a result of these agreements.

The failure of this approach leads us to ask: Is there a less costly and less dangerous way to provide nations with security?...

Three Paths to Peace

Two proposals which aim at making fundamental changes in the international security system illustrate the range of problems. The first is that made by Grenville Clark and Louis B. Sohn in their book *World Peace through World Law,* generally regarded as the most scholarly and comprehensive proposal for the general and complete disarmament of all nations. The second is the one drafted in 1961 by John J. McCloy and Valerian Zorin, "Joint Statement of Agreed Principles for Disarmament Negotiations," ratified unanimously by the U.N. General Assembly in 1962. I advocate a third approach, a defensive weapons system.

Since national security, from a military standpoint, is concerned with preventing hostile forces or weapons from crossing national boundaries, the two primary questions on which a new international security system will be judged are: What military forces will remain in the world after such a system is in effect? Who will control these forces? (A distinction is made throughout between military forces and lightly armed police forces required for internal order.)

Clark and Sohn propose a world peace force—the only military force to be left in the world—of between 200,000 and 400,000 regulars with a reserve of 300,000 to 600,000 equipped with conventional weapons. Nuclear weapons would be used only if authorized by a civilian authority and under the most unusual circumstances. . . . .

The McCloy-Zorin Agreement proposes to eliminate the military establishments of all nations, including "the disbanding

175

of armed forces, the dismantling of military establishments, including bases, the cessation of the production of armaments as well as their liquidation or conversion to peaceful uses." Further, it proposes "the elimination of all stockpiles of nuclear, chemical, bacteriological and other weapons of mass destruction, and the cessation of the production of such weapons; the elimination of all means of delivery of weapons of mass destruction; the abolition of organizations and institutions designed to organize the military effort of states, the cessation of military training, and the closing of all military training institutions; and the discontinuance of military expenditures." . . .

Defensive Weapons System

Over the last several years I have become convinced that the most feasible approach to reversing the arms race and drastically reducing the possibility of war is for all nations to limit their armaments to those that are useful only for defense. My reason is that the other approaches run into insurmountable roadblocks. The attempt to control and reduce armaments within an international security system based on military competition has been proven impractical. The notion of transferring effective military power and control of that power to a world authority has repeatedly met solid opposition from the Soviet Union and it is also quite doubtful that the United States would accept it. Implementation of the McCloy-Zorin principles would go a long way toward abolishing organized warfare but these principles are not clear on the two key issues of what military forces will remain and who will control them. The defensive weapons concept provides a resolution to these two issues that might be acceptable.

Simplicity is a key feature of the defensive weapons proposal. It is based on readily understandable and, in some respects, traditional concepts:

- Defense is good and offense is bad.
- Each nation retains absolute control.
- An effective inspection system is essential.

A most important aspect of the defensive weapons system is that it would greatly strengthen the security of the smaller as well as the larger nations. This is because the defensive capability of any nation is determined to a large extent by the offensive capabilities of its enemies. Under the present international security system, in which the arms competition between nations is virtually unrestrained, Mexico, for example, could not possibly withstand an all-out attack by the United

176

States. But if the United States had destroyed all offensive weapons and Mexico had built up her own defensive capability, then Mexico could make it very costly—perhaps impossible—for the United States to invade and occupy that country. Or, if the Soviet Union and Afghanistan had both adopted a defensive weapons system, the chances are that the Soviets would never have attempted an invasion.

A world in which the capacity for aggressive warfare had been eliminated—and this could be accomplished by 1990—would by no means resolve all the world's critical problems. But it would be a very different world from the one we have now.

A Change in Values

Where human societies are organized for the purpose of carrying on war (and there are few which are not), there is always the danger that war will occur. Universal changes both in organization in cultural ideals must take place in all important human societies before real progress can be made. The present situation, with the majority of civilized societies organized and capable of war, is a dangerous one. This situation is only hopeful in that all the major powers are now committed to the ideal of international peace.

John Paul Scott, *Aggression*, The University of Chicago Press.

It Can Work

The issues that appear so threatening to national interests would no longer seem so important. For example, the Soviets consider secrecy with respect to the positioning of weapons vital to their security, which makes agreement on adequate inspection virtually impossible. But with only defensive weapons, the location of missiles would no longer be an issue. Similarly, nations within the competitive armaments system are reluctant to have international disputes submitted to third parties since an adverse decision might affect their security. But a shift to defensive weapons would make legal procedures, arbitration and other non-violent ways of settling disputes seem far less threatening and more acceptable.

But is the defensive weapons proposal politically feasible? And what are the chances that many of the world's governments, including those of the superpowers, would take the idea seriously? Suppose one could prove beyond any reasonable doubt that an international security system based on defensive weapons would effectively eliminate the possibility of nuclear war; reduce global military expenditures by over $400 billion annually; enable national governments to reduce taxes, stop inflation and decentralize governmental functions. And suppose further that all this could happen without any sacrifice by the people of the world. There is still no assurance that it would happen. This is due not so much to the vested interests in the military-industrial complex as to the inability or unwillingness of world leaders to think freshly and act boldly.

Yet there are occasions when it is far easier to mobilize support to do the big job than to mobilize support for smaller steps which, on the surface, seem more achievable. The reason for this apparent contradiction is that the outcome of many complex, politically controversial issues is determined not so much by the difficulties that must be overcome but, even more important, by the possible rewards.

Moving from the competitive armaments system to a system of security based on defensive weapons will by no means create a utopia. But it would mark a historic change in our perception of the usefulness and functions of military establishments. At the same time, it would provide a period of reduced tensions necessary to develop the procedures and institutions required for a more stable and just peace.

"Necessary changes will come only when people . . . press government officials to end the deadly war system in favor of a global peace system."

A Peace System Can Eliminate War

Robert C. Johansen

Robert C. Johansen is Senior Fellow and Chairman of Research and Policy Studies at the World Policy Institute. He is the author of *The National Interest and the Human Interest: An Analysis of U.S. Foreign Policy*, as well as other monographs and articles on U.S. foreign policy and the nuclear arms buildup. He received his Ph.D. degree from Columbia University and has taught and conducted research at Manchester College and Princeton University. Currently, Dr. Johansen is Visiting Fellow at Princeton University's Center for International Studies and a member of the Board of Directors of the Arms Control Association. In the following viewpoint, he offers a unique proposal on how global peace may be achieved.

As you read, consider the following questions:

1. In what way does the author compare the invention of nuclear weapons to the invention of gunpowder?
2. What strategy does the author propose for achieving a demilitarized world?
3. Do you believe that the author's proposal can work? Why or why not?

Robert C. Johansen, *How to Avoid Death and Taxes*. Reprinted with permission of the World Policy Institute, New York, NY.

We are not secure right now. The military forces of the nation-state after the invention of nuclear weapons are like the castle after the invention of gunpowder. No matter how thick the walls centuries ago, no matter how heavy the defenses now, protection against attack is impossible. . . .

When gunpowder brought down castle walls, castle dwellers either had to abolish war or keep the users of gunpowder farther away. In fact, they did some of both. They abolished war among feudal lords and provincial monarchs by enlarging small kingdoms into nation-states. But war continued between nation-states.

Because it wasn't abolished completely, human insecurity sharply increased with the invention of nuclear weapons. National military forces, which had replaced the castle wall, became less effective for defense. Sensing our defenselessness, we and our government have acted like die-hard castle dwellers, and thickened the walls of the defenses. Our castle walls are now 50 nuclear layers thick. That is, the United States can destroy the Soviet Union 50 times over. . . .

Our Present Insecurity

Worse than that, to continue large military expenditures year after year *decreases* security. Our weapons are so effective that when other nations learn to copy them—which they always do—we find ourselves threatened by our own inventions. More than thirty countries can have nuclear weapons within ten years. The superpowers stockpile hundreds of new warheads annually, even though they already possess far more than required to destroy each other many times. If these weapons were fired, nobody in the Northern Hemisphere would be likely to survive. . . .

If the security and economic costs of military spending are so high, why don't we change our course? We and our military rivals are both caught in a military habit. We are likely addicts who turned to drugs to relieve anxiety and new need to increase the dose to feel secure. Real problems may have led to the addiction, but the habit itself becomes suicidal. . .

If our civilization is to survive, basic changes must take place that will enable us to break the military habit—which is the modern equivalent of the castle mentality. Until this habit is broken, certain weapons may come and go as SALT fails or succeeds, but like the addict's craving for a fix, arms buildups will always return. Only a new approach can save our cherished values.

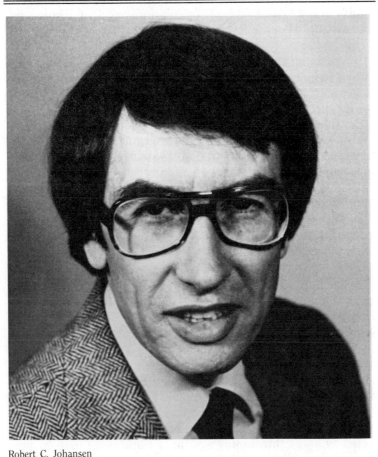

Robert C. Johansen

Our Present Opportunity

It is difficult to imagine a world without war, but no more difficult than to imagine a world after war. Because this difficulty has yet to be overcome, many people believe that war can never be eradicated. . . .

Today, instead of asking how to increase our capacity for destruction, we are rightly questioning: "Must there be a war system at all?"

A system based on war or the threat of force becomes unnecessary when we understand that on balance it undermines instead of increases our security. Security can be improved when a demilitarized world security system is established and military equipment for all countries' armed forces is strictly prohibited. A double monitoring system of national and global authorities would detect violations of prohibitions against arms, and a transnational peace force would enforce rules against rearmament. . . .

Despite general agreement with the preceding discussion, many people remain skeptical of any strategy for abolishing war as an acceptable institution. After all, what if an opponent cheats during the arms reduction process?

Consider whether the strategy proposed below may pose less risk to our security than indefinite continuation of the present arms competition. During the suggested process of reducing arms and establishing global monitoring agencies, governments will retain enough weapons to discourage an attack by another country and to make small differences in military power insignificant. Once agencies are firmly in place and arms are reduced, fear of being conquered will diminish. Although the major powers may remain rivals, they will no longer need to prepare for war.

If the United States takes the lead, Soviet officials will be likely to join this movement because it is in their self-interest. They want to avoid major war, the spread of nuclear weapons, and the economic burden of the war system. Once the process is under way, economic and diplomatic self-interest will strongly reinforce the movement to transform the war system. No plan, of course, can offer absolute guarantees against irrational behavior—least of all the present balance of terror which requires rational behavior by both sides if we are to avoid war. Irrational behavior is to be feared, but it is more likely to be corrected by a less threatening system of world order than by present military confrontations. The influence of more peaceful members of Soviet leadership would be strengthened by the steps proposed below.

Strategy for Change

If enough people replace their present silent support for today's uncertain security system with friendly but firm insistence on creating a more dependable one, the world community could become safe in several decades by taking the following steps:

Phase One: In this period, people committed to abolition of the war system will educate themselves and others about the dangers of the arms race and the urgent need for a peace system. They will advocate an understanding of security which includes economic health, basic human rights, and ecological balance, as well as a dependable world peace without national military arsenals. Their immediate goal will be to reduce U.S. and Soviet military spending annually by 10 percent of the previous year's expenditures.

Phase Two: Public pressure will build until the superpowers cut their military budgets by 10 percent each year. To dramatize its commitment to abolishing the war system, the United States can initiate the budget-reducing process, even without negotiations with the Soviet Union or any immediate response from it. These reductions can be made for two years without jeopardizing U.S. security, which will continue to depend on weapons previously purchased and maintained with the billions remaining in the military budget. Global and national monitoring agencies will begin to verify cutbacks, even if begun only by a few nations. This phase will end when both superpowers have made similar annual budget reductions for a five year period. Yearly budget cuts will continue through all the following phases.

Phase Three: The U.S. and U.S.S.R. will reduce their nuclear arms to the lowest level that still enables the destruction of the other side. Medium powers that have not joined the new security effort will be required to cut military outlays at the established pace. Demilitarized zones will expand as budgets are lowered.

Phase Four: Annual cuts in military expenditures will increase to 20 percent of each preceding year's budget. All states will now participate. Reductions will be verified with increasing precision by global and national agencies. Nuclear weapons will be completely dismantled, but conventional arms will remain.

Phase Five: Budget reductions will continue until military expenditures and national military arsenals are permanently prohibited at the end of this period. A global security organization will prevent rearmament.

To start the process for breaking the military habit, the United States can take the first initiatives and create incentives to convince other governments to participate. The United States can cut its military budget, suspend deployment of new weapons, and stop nuclear testing. We can safely take these initiatives and wait a reasonable time for the Soviet leaders to reciprocate, because our present nuclear forces exceed what will be required to offset Soviet deployments over the next several years. Such a sustained effort is needed to cut through the suspicion and habit built up during years of arms escalation.

Pressure from Below

Necessary changes will come only when people like you and me join other citizens to press government officials to end the deadly war system in favor of a global peace system. We must foster attitudes and institutions that recognize the link between genuine security and a demilitarized world. If left to follow their present habits, policymakers will continue the more than thirty years of arms control discussions which have failed to stop the arms buildup. Negotiators have sought to stabilize arms rather than to eliminate dependence on weapons. Arms control efforts focus on military inequalities and often trigger new arms efforts to close or increase gaps. If a SALT agreement is reached, it will legitimize existing arms and allow the deployment of even more destructive weapons.

Diplomats fail to lead us to a more secure, demilitarized world for yet another reason. Personal prestige and power come from the warfare system which now needs to be replaced. Consequently, our leaders continue familiar policies even though they lead to disaster. Progressive change seldom comes intentionally from the top without strong pressure from below.

3 VIEWPOINT

"The method of nonviolent resistance . . . does not leave a sense of frustration and it brings a more perfect peace."

Nonviolent Resistance Can Eliminate War

Richard B. Gregg

Richard B. Gregg, born in 1885, is a confirmed pacifist who is an ardent follower of the Ghandhi movement. He met with Mahatma Ghandhi in his early years, and has published many books on the theme of nonviolence since then. The following viewpoint is an excerpt from his book entitled *The Power of Nonviolence*. In it, Mr. Gregg demonstrates why nonviolence is similar to war in all but one important respect—little or no blood is shed.

As you read, consider the following questions:

1. In what ways, according to the author, does nonviolent resistance resemble war?
2. Why does the author believe that nonviolent resistance is more efficient than war?
3. The author believes that nonviolent resistance is a realistic path to peace. Do you agree? Why or why not?

Despite the horrors, futilities and destructiveness of war, there are nevertheless certain virtues and truths associated with it which humanity cannot afford to lose. In any discussion of new ways of settling conflicts, these military virtues cannot safely be disregarded.

Before the First World War, the romance and glamor of war was an undoubted fact, especially for those who never had taken part in war. The two world wars have destroyed all the glamor. Yet there is in all hearts a desire to live a significant life, to serve a great idea and sacrifice oneself for the noble cause, to feel the thrill of spiritual unity with one's fellows and to act in accordance therewith. We all wish for strenuous action and the exercise of courage and fortitude, to be carried away by the enthusiasm of daring. We all love to undergo a common dicipline and hardship for the sake of a fine ideal; to be in good effective order; to be strong, generous and self-reliant; to be physically fit, with body, mind and soul harmoniously working together for a great purpose, thus becoming a channel of immense energies. Under such conditions, the whole personality is alert, conscious, unified and living profoundly, richly and exaltedly. Then one can be truly and gloriously happy. Martial music suggests many of these elements and their consequent exhilaration and exaltation. . .

All these virtues and truths of war are given full scope and exercise in the nonviolent method of settling great disputes. If any nation or group adopts mass nonviolent resistance, no moral losses will result. . .

Nonviolent Warfare

We see that nonviolent resistance resembles war in these eight ways:

(1) It has a psychological and moral aim and effect,
(2) It is a discipline of a parallel emotion and instinct,
(3) It operates against the morale of the opponents,
(4) It is similar in principles of strategy,
(5) It is a method of settling great disputes and conflicts,
(6) It requires courage, dynamic energy, capacity to endure fatigue and suffering, self-sacrifice, self-control, chivalry, action,
(7) It is positive and powerful,
(8) It affords an opportunity of service for a large idea, and for glory.

It does not avoid hardships, suffering, wounds or even death. In using it men and women may still risk their lives and fortunes and sacrifice all. Nevertheless the possibilities of casualties and death are greatly reduced under it, and they are all suffered voluntarily and not imposed by the nonviolent resisters.

In [Gandhi's] struggle for independence, though I know of no accurate statistics, hundreds of thousands of Indians went to jail, probably not more than five hundred received permanent physical injuries, and probably not over eight thousand were killed immediately or died later from wounds. No British, I believe, were killed or wounded. Considering the importance and size of the conflict and the many years it lasted, these numbers are much smaller than they would have been if the Indians had used violence toward the British.

Nonviolent resistance is more efficient than war because it costs far less in money as well as in lives and suffering. Also it usually permits a large part of the agricultural and industrial work of the people to go on, and hence the life of the country can be maintained during the struggle.

It is again more efficient than war because "the legitimate object of war is a more perfect peace." If the peace after the war

---

The Principle of *Satyagraha*

Philosophers and peace lovers are earnestly in search of a moral equivalent of war that would embody the technical features of war minus its violence as the surest way to establish peace. The technique of *satyagraha* proposed by Gandhi with a view to meet the challenge of war operates on the basis of nonviolence. The guiding principle in his approach is that the means must be as good as the end. Since the means-end relation forms one continuous process, no true good can result from an immoral means: hence the appropriateness of nonviolent resistance as the alternative to war.

R. Balasubramanian, from *The Critique of War*, ed. by Robert Ginsberg.

---

is to be better than that which preceded it, the psychological processes of the conflict must be such as will create a more perfect peace. You can't climb a mountain by constantly going downhill. Mutual violence inevitably breeds hatred, revenge and bitterness—a poor foundation for a more perfect peace. The method of nonviolent resistance, where there really is resistance, so as to bring all the issues out into the open, and the working out of a really new settlement, as nearly as possible in accord with the full truth of the issues at stake—this method does not leave a sense of frustration and it brings a more perfect peace.

187

A Universal Weapon

Considering the completeness of its effects, nonviolent resis
tance is as quick and probably quicker than war. It is a weapon
that can be used equally well by small or large nations or groups,
by the economically weak and by the apparently strong, and
even by individuals. It compels both sides and neutrals to seek
the truth, whereas war blinds both sides and neutrals to the
truth.

As we have already seen and will show further, nonviolent
resistance certainly produces less ill-effects, if any, than war
does, and this decrease of ill-effects applies to the users of nonviolence, to the opposing side, and to society and the world
at large.

It is interesting to note that in early 1958 there was published
a book by a British naval officer (not a pacifist), Commander Sir
Stephen King-Hall, in which he argues that nonviolent resistance is now the best and only possible successful mode of
defense of Great Britain against armed attack. He argues the
points in detail and cogently: "We must," he says, "ask ourselves
this question: 'If the contribution of violence (i.e., military
operations) to the settlement of differences of opinion or conflicts (werre) between sovereign states has evolved to such intensity that it is totally destructive, has not violence outlived its
usefulness in disputes between large states?' It looks to me as if
this is the truth. Bearing in mind that in major disputes violence
has become equated with nuclear energy violence, I am forced to
consider what possibilities are open to us if we exclude violence
from our defense plans on the grounds that violence has become
our master instead of our slave." Many other keen thinkers all
through the West agree that nuclear weapons have destroyed the
effectiveness of war as a means to settle large disputes
between nations.

May we not then fairly describe nonviolent resistance as an
effective substitute for war?

It is realistic in that it does not eliminate or attempt to
eliminate possiblities of conflict and differences of interest, and
includes all factors in the situation — both material and impon-
derable, physical and psychological. A British psychologist
argues that the fundamental reasons for war are sadism and
masochism, and that, until these deepseated urges are modified,
war cannot be ended. In so far as sadism and masochism are per-
verted expressions of a desire for power, however, nonviolent
resistance can control them by substituting its own method of

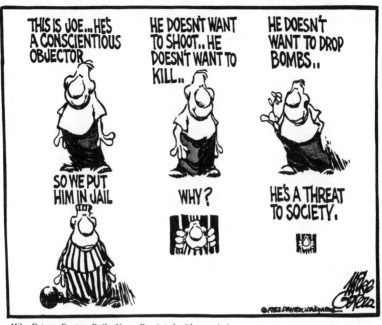

Mike Peters, *Dayton Daily News*. Reprinted with permission.

securing a power that is much greater and more satisfying.

A New Kind of War

It does not require any nation to surrender any part of its real sovereignty or right of decision, as a world government might. It does not surrender the right of self-defense, although it radically alters the nature of the defense. It requires no expensive weapons or armament, no drill grounds or secrecy. It does not demoralize those who take part in it, but leaves them finer men and women than when the struggle began.

Moreover, the method does not require the machinery of a government or a large wealthy organization. It may be practiced and skill may be acquired in it in every situation of life, at home and abroad, by men and women of any and all races, nations, tribes, groups, classes or castes, young and old, rich and poor. That women take part in it is important. Indeed, they are more effective in it than most men.

In as much as some of the elements involved are essentially the same as trust, they have the same energizing effect as financial credit, only more so. Thus it stimulates and mobilizes, during the conflict and for a long time thereafter, all the idealism and energy of all groups and parties. . .

May we not therefore say of it in the words which Marshal Foch used in reference to a different occasion: "The new kind of war has begun, the hearts of soldiers have become a new weapon."

"Civil-based defense could break the technological weaponry spiral, and bypass the major problems of negotiated disarmament and arms control agreements."

Civil-Based Defense Can Eliminate War

Gene Sharp

Gene Sharp is program director of the Program on Nonviolent Sanctions in Conflict and Defense, Harvard University's Center for International Affairs. He received his doctorate in philosophy from Oxford University and is now professor of political science and sociology at Southeastern Massachusetts University. Dr. Sharp is the author of several books and is an international lecturer. In the following viewpoint, he unveils a somewhat unusual mechanism for peace, one which he terms "civil-based defense."

As you read, consider the following questions:

1. What does the author mean by civilian-based defense?
2. According to the author, how is civilian-based defense relevant to the problem of nuclear weapons?
3. Do you believe that civilian-based defense can work? Why or why not?

Gene Sharp, *Making the Abolition of War A Realistic Goal.* Reprinted with permission of the World Policy Institute, New York, NY and the author.

Peace proposals and movements of the past have failed to offer a credible alternative defense policy in place of war. Therefore, whether they instead offered as solutions to the problem of war negotiations, compromises, conciliation, international conferences, supranational leagues, or anti-war resistance, their common failure could have been predicted.

On the other hand, the stubborn persistence of advocates of strong defense in considering only military means and failing to investigate nonmilitary possibilities has led to the present dangerous situation and to the lack of development of possible options.

If we want to reduce drastically, or remove, reliance on war and other types of violent conflict it is necessary to substitute a nonviolent counterpart of war, "war without violence," by which people can defend liberty, their way of life, humanitarian principles, their institutions and society, at least as effectively against military attack as can military means.

Such a substitute defense policy would need to be one which can be (1) held in reserve to encourage settlements without resort to open struggle (as by facilitating settlements, reducing misperceptions, and deterring aggression by effective defense capacity as such) and (2) used effectively in an open defense struggle against attack. ("Defense" here must be understood literally, as protection, warding off of danger, preservation, and the like. Defense is therefore not necessarily tied to military means, and has been provided by nonmilitary forms of struggle.) . . .

Civilian-Based Defense

This alternative policy of deterrence and defense is called "civilian-based defense." That is a defense policy which utilizes prepared civilian struggle—nonviolent action—to preserve the society's freedom, sovereignty, and constitutional system against internal usurpations and external invasions and occupations. The aim is to deter to defeat such attacks. This is to be done not simply by efforts to alter the will of the attacker, but by the capacity to make effective domination and control impossible by both massive and selective nonviolent noncooperation and defiance by the population and its institutions. The aim is to make the populace unrulable by the attackers and to deny them their objectives. A genuine capacity to do that, if accurately perceived, could deter both internal takeovers and foreign invasions.

It is possible to exert extreme pressure and even to coerce by nonviolent means. Rather than converting the opponent, civilian struggle has more often been waged by disrupting, paralyzing, or coercing the opponent by denying the cooperation he needed, and upsetting the normal operation of the system. This is a foundation for civilian-based strategies.

An attack for ideological and indoctrination purposes, for example, would likely involve noncooperation and defiance by schools, newspapers, radio, television, churches, all levels of government, and the general population, to reject the indoctrination attempts, and reassertion of democratic principles.

An attack aimed at economic exploitation would be met with economic resistance — boycotts, strikes, noncooperation by experts, management, transport workers and officials — aimed at reducing, dissolving or reversing any economic gains to the attackers.

Coups d'état and executive usurpations would be met with noncooperation of civil servants, bureaucrats, government agencies, state and local government, police departments, and virtually all the social institutions and general populations as a whole, to deny legitimacy, and to prevent consolidation of effective control by the usurpers over the government and society.

Defense Responsibilities

Various population groups and institutions would have responsibility for particular defense tasks, depending on the exact issues at stake.

For example, police whould refuse to locate and arrest patriotic resisters against the attacker. Journalists and editors refusing to submit to censorship would publish newspapers illegally in large editions or many small editions — as happened in the Russian 1905 Revolution and in several Nazi-occupied countries. Free radio programs would continue from hidden transmitters — as happened in Czechoslovakia in 1968.

Clergymen would preach the duty to refuse help to the invader — as happened in the Netherlands under the Nazis.

Politicans, civil servants, judges, and the like by ignoring or defying the enemy's illegal orders, would keep the normal machinery of government, the courts, etc., out of his control — as happened in the German resistance to the Kapp *Putsch* in 1920.

The judges would declare the invader's officials an illegal and unconstitutional body, continue to operate on the basis of pre-invasion laws and constitutions, and refuse to give moral support to the invader, even if they had to close the courts.

Teachers would refuse to introduce propaganda into the schools—as happened in Norway under the Nazis. Attempts to control schools could be met with refusal to change the school curriculum or to introduce the invader's propaganda, explanations to the pupils of the issues at stake, continuation of regular education as long as possible, and, if necessary, closing the schools and holding private classes in the children's homes.

Workers and managers would impede exploitation of the country by selective strikes, delays, and obstructionism—as happened in the Ruhr in 1923.

Attempts to control professional groups and trade unions could be met by persistence in abiding by their pre-invasion constitutions and procedures, refusal to recognize new organizations set up by the invader, refusal to pay dues or attend meetings of any new pro-invader organizations, and the wielding of disruptive strikes, managerial defiance and obstruction, and economic and political boycotts.

These defense tasks are only illustrative of a multitude of specific forms of defense action which would be possible. Civilian-based defense operates not only on the principle that the price of liberty is eternal vigilance, but that defense of independence and freedom is the responsibility of every citizen.

This is a more total type of defense than the military system, since it involves the whole population and all its institutions in defense struggle. Because such participation must be voluntary in order to be reliable in crises, and because of reliance on nonviolent means, however, civilian-based defense is intrinsically democratic.

As in military warfare, this type of struggle is applied in face of violent enemy action. Casualties are—as in military struggle—to be expected. In this case, however, they are utilized to advance the cause of the defenders (as by increasing their resistance) and to undermine the opponent's power (as by alienating his own supporters). There is no more reason to be dismayed by casualties, or to capitulate when they occur, than there is when they occur in military conflict. In fact, it appears that casualties in civilian struggles are far lower than in military conflicts. . . .

Nuclear Weapons

Major attention is required in consideration of this policy to its possible relevance or limitations in relation to nuclear weapons. This field has not yet been adequately examined. It is

194

possible, on the one hand, that civilian-based defense may be developed to be an adequate substitute for conventional military defense, but be irrelevant to the nuclear question. In that case, nuclear weapons would need to be dealt with by other means, such as arms control treaties, other international controls, unilateral initiatives to reduce reliance on nuclear weapons, or even unilateral dismantling of them as sources of greater danger than safety.

On the other hand, civilian-based defense may be relevant to the problem of nuclear weapons in several indirect ways. For example, a country with a civilain based defense policy and without nuclear armed rockets aimed at other nuclear powers.

Gene Sharp

In a different context, the massive buildup of so-called "tactical" nuclear weapons in Western Europe to be used in case of a Soviet Blitzkrieg westward is premised on the incapacity of N.A.T.O. forces to defend Western Europe sucessfully by conventional military means. Thoroughly prepared civilian-based defense policies in Western European countries, by their capacity to ensure a massive and continuing defense struggle capable of maintaining the autonomy of the attacked societies . . . would constitute a more powerful deterrent and defense policy than can conventional military means. Therefore, the reliance on nuclear weapons to deter and defend against a Soviet attack on Western Europe would not be required. . . .

Creating a Choice

Civilian-based defense could break the technological weaponry spiral, and bypass the major problems of negotiated disarmament and arms control agreements. With full recognition of international and domestic dangers, whole countries could mobilize effective capacities to prevent, deter, and defend against attacks—while at the same time reducing, and finally abandoning, reliance on military means.

For the first time, therefore, it becomes possible in advance of crises to choose between reliance on military capacity to deter and defend against attack and reliance on an alternative to war for the same purposes. Without such a choice between two or more policies to deter attacks and defend against them, overwhelmingly, with only the possibility of rare exceptions, most people and governments will cling to war. They do not really have a choice.

With the development of a choice, the future course of events hinges to a significant degree on the extent to which the civilian-based defense option is in fact adequate to the defense tasks and also on the preception of its adequacy. Therefore, the advance basic research, problem-solving research, policy studies, feasibility studies, preparations, contingency planning, and training are of extreme importance. So also are the population's defense will, the resilience of the society's non-State institutions in resistance, and the skill of the civilian defenders in formulating and implementing wise strategies. Advance identification of possible objectives of potential internal usurpers and foreign attackers and of vulnerable points in such groups and regimes will also be important. . . .

Although some countries might never abandon military means entirely, demonstrations that aggression does not pay and can be defeated could limit the harm they could do. Other countries, however, could increasingly move, by adoption of a substitute for military defense, to abandon war as an instrument of national policy. This could lead progressively toward the removal of military power and war as a major factor in international relations.*

*The author has requested that the following information be offered to the reader:
Gene Sharp's books include the following titles available from Porter Sargent Publishers, 11 Beacon St., Boston, MA 01208: The Politics of Nonviolent Action (1973); paperback in three volumes: I, Power and Struggle, $2.95; II, The Methods of Nonviolent Action, $4.95; III, The Dynamics of Nonviolent Action, $5.95; Gandhi as a Political Strategist, with Essays on Ethics and Politics (1979), $7.95; Social Power and Political Freedom (1980), $8.95.

"The United States could now take unilateral actions that would . . . increase the safety of the . . . rest of the world."

Unilateral Action Can Bring Peace

Linus Pauling

Nobel Prize laureate Linus Pauling has focused his life on resolving world conflict and achieving world peace. In this endeavor, he is the recipient of the US Presidential Medal for Merit, the International Lenin Peace Prize, and other honorary degrees and awards. Dr. Pauling, who was born in 1901, current-ly heads the Institute of Science and Medicine in Palo Alto, California. In the following viewpoint, he explains why he believes that unilateral actions by the US would be a decided step toward world peace.

As you read, consider the following questions:

1. What does the author mean when he writes that the U.S. "took the unilateral action . . . in the wrong direction"?
2. What is the position of the Boston Study Group regard-ing disarmament?
3. What is your opinion of the type of "unilateral action" advocated by the author?

This viewpoint is excerpted from an address presented at the 25th anniversary of the Pugwash meet-ing, Pugwash, Nova Scotia, July 16-19, 1982.

For many years I have advocated that progress toward control of nuclear weapons, achievement of world peace, general disarmament, and the international cooperation be made by means of treaties, especially between the United States and the Soviet Union. In my book, *No More War!*, published in 1958, I wrote that "The time has now come for war to be abandoned, for diplomacy to move out of the 19th century into the real world of the 20th century, a world in which war and the threat of war no longer have a rightful place as the instrument of national policy. We must move toward a world governed by justice, by international law, and not by force. We must all, including the diplomats and national leaders, change our point of view. We must recognize that extreme nationalism is a thing of the past. The idea that it is just as important to do harm to other nations as to do good for your own nation must be given up. We must all begin to work for the world as a whole, for humanity.

The Wrong Direction

I now believe that we can reach the goal by unilateral action — by a series of unilateral actions by the United States, the Soviet Union, and other countries, supplemented by international agreements as rapidly as they can be formulated and ratified.

I should like to see the United States take the lead in this process. The United States has been in the lead, ever since 1945, when we exploded our nuclear bombs over Hiroshima and Nagasaki. We have continued to be in the lead, although before long the situation had become such as to make it essentially meaningless to ask whether one country or the other was ahead in the power of destruction.

In fact, the United States has been taking unilateral actions throughout this entire period, but almost always in the wrong direction. Our representatives and those of the Soviet Union negotiated for seven years in order to formaulate the SALT II treaty. We then took the unilateral action of refusing to ratify it — an action in the wrong direction. We introduced MIRV, and a few years later the Soviet Union was also equipping her rockets with multiple warheads. We are now considering an increase in the number of our nuclear weapons by 14,000. We have, unilaterally, developed the Cruise missile. I do not need to quote all of the examples.

I think that the United States could now take unilateral actions that would greatly reduce the amount of military spending and, at the same time, increase the safety of the United

States and of the rest of the world.

The way in which this could be done is discussed in detail in the book, *The Price of Defense: A New Strategy for Military Spending,* by the Boston Group-Randall Forsberg, Martin Moore-Ede, Philip Morrison, Phylis Morrison, George Sommaripa, and Paul F. Walker. One unilateral step toward disarmament could be taken by the United States, and we could see whether or not the Soviet Union follows by taking a similar step.

I believe that the pressure on the Soviet Union to decrease the spending on armaments is greater than that on the United States, because the armaments expenditures represent a greater percentage of the wealth of the nation. Also, I am sure that the Soviet people and the Soviet government are more afraid of war than are the people and the government of the United States, because the Soviet people have experienced wars in a way that we have not.

The Boston Study Group advocates decrease in the destructive power of nuclear weapons from the present completely-insane level to a less-irrational level, still great enough to serve as a deterrent to the Third World War. By their detailed analysis they showed that their policy would not only save tremendous amounts of money but would also greatly decrease the probability of world destruction.

Jerome Wiesner begins his essay with the paragraph, "There is an easily-structured, effective way to stop the escalating arms race. President Reagan should declare an open-ended unilateral moratorium, always subject to reversal, on the production, testing, and deployment of new nuclear weapons and delivery systems. He should invite the Russians to respond with a parallel declaration of purpose. If they did, it would result in a non-negotiated freeze. Only the president has the power and prestige to put this into effect; only he might have the courage to break such new ground and help reduce worldwide fear. . . . The challenge is to action, not negotiation. Once both countries have declared a moratorium, either can take the initiative to go further and further along the path. A moratorium, to be acceptable, must be safe for everyone—for us, for the Soviet Union, and for both sides' allies. Is a moratorium safe? I believe that it is. . . . A moratorium does not have to mean 'stop everything.' . . . It is important to understand what a moratorium is and, especially, what it is not. It is not nuclear disarmament. It is a way of arresting the arms race. It is a unilateral path to a freeze. . . . The unilateral moratorium should be just a first step in global psychotherapy."

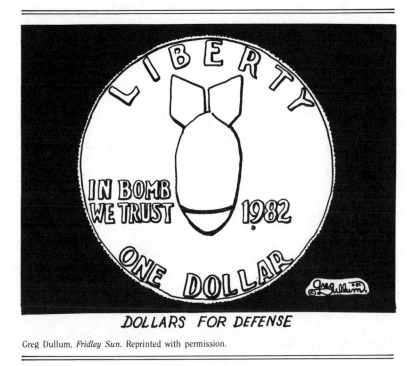

DOLLARS FOR DEFENSE

Greg Dullum, *Fridley Sun*. Reprinted with permission.

The Necessary Step

I believe that we can overcome the irrational drive toward race suicide.

I believe that human beings in the United States and the Soviet Union can cooperate to solve the great problems we face.

Nineteen years ago I said that "War and nationalism, together with economic exploitation, have been great enemies of the individual human being. I believe that, with war abolished from the world, there will be improvement in the social, political, and economic systems in all nations, to the benefit of the whole of humanity."

I suggest that we consider issuing a manifesto recommending that the great nations begin to take unilateral steps toward world peace and a rational future.

"Today a peace academy should be an even more compelling idea than it was to the founding fathers."

A Peace Academy Can Promote Peace

Don & Lynn Leverty

In 1981, Senator Spark Matsunaga (D-Hawaii) introduced a bill that would establish a U.S. Academy of Peace. The following viewpoint, authored by Don and Lynn Leverty, attempts to explain why such an Academy is a timely and potentially fruitful idea. Mr. Leverty holds a Master's degree in Journalism from the University of Kansas and is a member of the staff of the chancellor of the University of Texas System. Ms. Leverty holds a Ph.D. in International Relations from American University, Washington, DC. A legislative assistant to former Representative Michael Harrington (D-Massachusetts), she currently is an aide to Governor Mark White of Texas.

As you read, consider the following questions:

1. Which national legislators introduced bills to establish a US Academy of Peace?
2. What three major functions would a peace academy perform?
3. What are some of the arguments presented by the authors favoring a peace academy?

"At Last, Why Not a School for Peace?" Lynn H. & Don Leverty, *Christian Science Monitor*, December 24, 1981. Reprinted with permission of the authors.

It was first proposed at the close of the Revolutionary War. Some historians attribute the idea to Dr. Benjamin Rush, a signer of the Declaration of Independence.

It is known that George Washington advanced a similar idea.

Neither plan for a federal "Peace Office" was implemented, and it wasn't until 1935 that someone finally introduced a bill in Congress that would have established such an agency.

Now a majority of the Senate thinks it is an idea whose time has come.

A bill introduced by Sen. Spark Matsunaga (D) of Hawaii, and cosponsored by 52 of his colleagues, would establish a US Academy of Peace—an academic center that would provide an intellectual and philosophical counterpoint to West Point. . . .

Rep. Dan Glickman (R) of Kansas introduced a companion bill in the House, where it received 55 cosponsors. He says a peace academy would acknowledge "the fact that growing world tensions cannot be controlled by military might alone."

The proposed center would serve leaders in government, private enterprise, and voluntary associations. It would perform three major functions:

• Research on peacemaking techniques such as negotiating and enforcing cease-fires and mediating disputes through United Nations offices;

• Education and training, including graduate and postgraduate credits, short-term courses for government and private personnel on negotiation, mediation and arbitration of international conflicts, and one-day conferences on topics such as negotiation and international terrorism;

• Information services—disseminating research findings through newsletters and pamphlets, establishing links with local libraries, and perhaps publishing a scholarly journal.

The facility would be a federally chartered nonprofit corporation located in or near Washington. Its core budget would come from federal funds, but it would also solicit supplemental private funding.

The academy would not intervene in international conflicts or attempt to set national policies. It is designed to provide a "coordinated national commitment to peace learning," which its supporters say is necessary to increase the effectiveness of our foreign and defense policymaking.

Senator Matsunaga, who earned the Bronze Star and two Purple Hearts in World War II, noted in a speech to the Senate that the cost of establishing the academy and running it for the first three years would be $31 million, less than one-tenth the price tag of a single B-1 bomber, based on moderate cost estimates.

The Pentagon already spends more than $10 billion a year to teach the arts of war; it runs three service academies, five military war colleges, and five more similar schools for its officers.

A Time for Change

Humanity's tragic propensity to rely on the most primitive

and counterproductive form of defense—violence or the threat of it—has endured since prehistory, but it now threatens the species.

This is not to say that the Soviets or our other adversaries are really peace-loving sheep in wolves' clothing. It is to say, however, that too little time and effort has been spent on serious study of alternatives to Armageddon.

American foreign-policy makers have not been able to adjust to a more complex world in which control of natural resources is shifting to the third world and many of our allies are faced with internal unrest. They tend to approach these economic and political currents as military problems, attacking complex problems with a blunt object.

We owe it to ourselves to find a better way.

Such a center would not have to plow totally new ground. It would draw on the science of conflict resolution and evaluate and disseminate information on the numerous unheralded examples of successful peacemaking around the world.

The National Peace Academy Campaign likes to quote the late Gen. Omar Bradley, the former US Army chief of staff and World War II hero: "We have become a nation of nuclear giants and ethical infants. We know more about war than we do about peace, more about killing that we do about living."

Today a peace academy should be an even more compelling idea than it was to the founding fathers.

Distinguishing Bias from Reason

The subject of war and peace often generates great emotional responses in people. When dealing with such a highly controversial subject, many will allow their feelings to dominate their powers of reason. Thus, one of the most important basic thinking skills is the ability to distinguish between opinions based upon emotion or bias and conclusions based upon a rational consideration of the facts.

Most of the following statements are taken from the viewpoints in this chapter. The rest are taken from other sources. Consider each statement carefully. *Mark R for any statement you believe is based on reason or a rational consideration of the facts. Mark B for any statement you believe is based on bias, prejudice or emotion. Mark I for any statement you think is impossible to judge.*

If you are doing this activity as the member of a class or group compare your answers with those of other class or group members. Be able to defend your answers. You may discover that others will come to different conclusions than you. Listening to the rationale others present for their answers may give you valuable insights in distinguishing between bias and reason.

If you are reading this book alone, ask others if they agree with your answers. You too will find this interaction very valuable.

> R = *a statement based upon reason*
> B = *a statement based on bias*
> I = *a statement impossible to judge*

1. The most feasible approach to reversing the arms race and drastically reducing the possibility of war is for all nations to limit their armaments to those that are useful only for defense.

2. The Soviets consider secrecy with respect to the positioning of weapons vital to their security, which makes agreement on adequate inspection virtually impossible.

3. If the security and economic costs of military spending are so high, why don't we change our course?

4. The major problem is twofold: There will always be wars and you can't change human nature.

5. When war becomes unprofitable, war will be eliminated.

6. Nonviolent resistance operates against the morale of one's opponents.

7. Nonviolent resistance would only work if *all* people were kind, cooperative and gentle.

8. Warfare is, in one sense, good for humanity. It helps separate the weak from the strong.

9. Although some countries might never abandon military means entirely, demonstrations that aggression does not pay and can be defeated could limit the harm they could do.

10. War can be avoided only in a world governed by justice, international law and not by force.

11. I believe that human beings in the U.S. and USSR can cooperate to solve the great problems we face.

12. We know more about war than we do about peace, more about killing than we do about living.

13. Humanity owes it to itself to find a lasting road to peace.

14. If the entire world were Christian and adhered to Christian principles, there would be peace.

Bibliography

The following list of books deals with the subject matter of this chapter.

Abrecht, Paul and Koshv, Ninan, eds.	*Before It's Too Late: The Challenge of Nuclear Disarmament*, Geneva, Switzerland: World Council of Churches, 1983.
Albert, Stuart and Luck, Edward C., eds.	*On the Endings of Wars*, Port Washington, NY: Kennikat Press Corp., 1980.
Ardley, Neil	*Future War and Weapons*, New York: Franklin Watts, Inc., 1982.
Bailey, Sydney D.	*How Wars End: The United Nations and the Termination of Armed Conflict*, New York: Oxford University Press, 1982.
Camus, Albert	*Neither Victims nor Executioners*, New York: Continuum Publishing Corp., 1980.
Clarke, Michael and Mowlam, Morjorie, eds.	*Debate on Disarmament*, Boston: Routledge and Kegan Paul, 1982.
Crosser, Paul K.	*War Is Obsolete: The Dialectics of Military Technology and Its Consequences*, Atlantic Highland, NJ: Humanities Press, Inc., 1972.
Dennis, Lawrence	*The Dynamics of War and Revolution*, Torrance, CA: Noontide Press, 1980.
Eller, Vernard	*War and Peace from Genesis to Revelation*, Scottdale, PA: Herald Press, 1981.
Fallows, James	*National Defense*, New York: Random House, 1981.
Heyer, Robert	*Nuclear Disarmament*, New York: Paulist Press, 1982.
Howe, Frederic C.	*Why War*, Seattle, WA: University of Washington Press, 1970.
Nickerson, Hoffman	*Can We Limit War?* Port Washington, NY: Kennikat Press Corp., 1973.
Thompson, W. Scott, ed.	*From Weakness to Strength: National Security in the 1980s*, San Francisco: Institute for Contemporary Studies, 1980.
Wallis, Jim	*Waging Peace*, New York: Harper & Row, 1982.

Index

212

The Editors

David L. Bender is a history graduate from the Univerity of Minnesota. He also has an M.A. in government from St. Mary's University in San Antonio, Texas. He has taught social problems at the high school level for several years. He is the general editor of the *Opposing Viewpoints Series* and has authored many of the titles in the series.

Bruno Leone received his B.A. (Phi Kappa Phi) from Arizona State University and his M.A. in history from the University of Minnestoa. A Woodrow Wilson Fellow (1967), he is currently an instructor at Minneapolis Community College, Minneapolis, Minnesota, where he has taught history, anthropology, and political science. In 1974-75, he was awarded a Fellowship by the National Endowment for the Humanities to research the intellectual origins of American Democracy. He has authored numerous titles in the *Opposing Viewpoints Series*.